Sermons from a Potato Field

Sermons from a Potato Field

Edgar Stubbersfield

Foreword by Alan Gordon

RESOURCE *Publications* · Eugene, Oregon

SERMONS FROM A POTATO FIELD

Copyright © 2022 Edgar Stubbersfield. All rights reserved. Except for brief quotations in critical publications or reviews, no part of this book may be reproduced in any manner without prior written permission from the publisher. Write: Permissions, Wipf and Stock Publishers, 199 W. 8th Ave., Suite 3, Eugene, OR 97401.

Resource Publications
An Imprint of Wipf and Stock Publishers
199 W. 8th Ave., Suite 3
Eugene, OR 97401

www.wipfandstock.com

PAPERBACK ISBN: 978-1-6667-4803-1
HARDCOVER ISBN: 978-1-6667-4804-8
EBOOK ISBN: 978-1-6667-4805-5

11/04/22

Scripture quotations taken from the (NASB®) New American Standard Bible®, Copyright © 1960, 1971, 1977, 1995, 2020 by The Lockman Foundation. Used by permission. All rights reserved. www.lockman.org

This book is dedicated to the faithful and capable men and women of Tenthill Baptist Church and their children, who, it is our earnest prayer, will become the next generation of believers.

Contents

Foreword by Alan Gordon | ix
Acknowledgments | xi
Introduction | xiii

1. To a Church in Drought | 1
2. Eternity in Our Hearts | 10
3. The Dark Night of the Soul | 19
4. The Farmer and the Theologian | 26
5. On Appointing a New Pastor | 33
6. On the Separation of Church and State | 40
7. Victorious Christian Living | 49
8. Sinners in the Hands of a Gracious God | 58
9. The Temple of Artemis | 64
10. Sermon on the Election of Church Officers | 72
11. Repent from Your Wicked Ways | 78
12. The Best Use of Life is Love | 84
13. Giving the Shirt Off Your Back | 91
14. Sermon Following the Boxing Day Tsunami | 97
15. Reflections on the Death of a Young Man | 103

16 The Lying Baptists | 108
17 My Cup Does Not Overflow | 114
18 Unswearing an Oath of Allegiance | 120
19 Psalm 85 | 123
20 My Socks Tell the Gospel | 130
21 Life's Storms | 131
22 The Parable of Hank | 136

Source of Images | 145

Foreword

What a title for a book of sermons!

When you have been a friend of Ted Stubbersfield for years, the title, and the contents, remain fresh expressions of the Word of God as I read Ted's sermons.

When I was pastor for Ted's church, I appreciated his warmth of friendship and his fresh approach to God's Word. I believed that Ted should be given a chance to preach a sermon.

Ted's sermons were immersed in Scripture and made relevant by illustrations created fresh and relevant by the content in which he was plunged in his daily life.

Ted was one of Australia's most creative, developers of beautiful designs of wood bridges and other weather-exposed timber structures and landscaping.

With his inbuilt culture of his worksite, Ted developed eyes for the farms in which he was immersed. He linked local culture's sights and sounds with the pure truths of God's Word. This same model of preaching was standard approach in the Bible itself by Ezekiel, David, Solomon, Elijah, Elisha, John the Baptist, Paul, and the Lord Jesus Himself.

The congregation loved his approach and the church was refreshed with the relevance of the Word of God to their daily lives.

When you read this book, capture the relevance of what contribution it can make by its Biblical truth and daily relevance.

Warm Christian greetings,

Dr Alan Gordon

Acknowledgments

I would like to acknowledge Barry Benz who tried to teach me to preach way back in 1972. He and his wife Elka have been close friends since and encouraged in me the hope of seeing revival.

Also, I would like to acknowledge Alan Gordon, a former pastor of Tenthill Baptist Church who prompted me to take up my studies again. The friendship he and Rosemary offered has been wonderful

Introduction

When I was sixteen, life as I knew it ceased and along with it my plans for the future. I had my first epileptic attack. It almost killed me. For the next ten years it would dominate my life as I went through times when it was virtually uncontrollable.

The particular type I have wiped out my abilities with foreign languages, preventing me from ever being a theologian and also prevented me flying for Missionary Aviation Fellowship. It is only through a computer with spell check that you can read my writing. But there have been positives! My brain appears to be wired differently which sometimes allows me to look at things differently. I produced a range of innovative products and had a number of patents when I operated my business. It also means that, for good or ill, I can view scriptures differently.

The sermons that follow were given by me and two guest contributors, all laymen, to the members of a small country church situated in a potato field in the farming community of Tenthill, in Queensland, Australia. After I had completed a number of academic books, a previous pastor at our church, Rev. Dr. Alan Gordon, asked me to also produce this book of sermons. I said to Alan, "They are different, aren't they?" He replied that they are very different and refreshing, but you can be the judge of that. This is not like a collection of sermons in a minister annual but are real sermons to real people in a real locality to meet real circumstances. The sermons are in no particular order and their layout varies. Generally, these sermons seemed to meet needs and were appreciated. I hope they bless you also.

I have two more books of sermons from the potato field, *Lettuce Pray* and *Twenty-four Carrot Faith*.

1

To a Church in Drought

Background

PARTS OF AUSTRALIA WENT through a protracted drought through the first years of the twenty-first century. Our creek did not run for ten years. The farming community that relied on extensive irrigation from a vast underground basin was devastated when this reserve failed. These were very hard years for our members.

The drought ended with a flood; the likes of which had never been seen before. Grantham, the closest town to the church was hit with an "inland tsunami" and many lost their lives. The farms further up the valley could not get their produce to market as the roads were simply destroyed. Repairs were still being carried out two years later.

Reading

Proverbs 31:10–31, The virtuous woman.

Text: Ruth 1:16–22

⁶ *But Ruth said, "Do not plead with me to leave you or to turn back from following you; for where you go, I will go, and where you sleep, I will sleep.*

Your people shall be my people, and your God, my God. ¹⁷ *Where you die, I will die, and there I will be buried. May the Lord do so to me, and worse, if anything but death separates me from you."* ¹⁸ *When she saw that she was determined to go with her, she stopped speaking to her about it.*

¹⁹ *So they both went on until they came to Bethlehem. And when they had come to Bethlehem, all the city was stirred because of them, and the women said, "Is this Naomi?"* ²⁰ *But she said to them, "Do not call me Naomi; call me Mara, for the Almighty has dealt very bitterly with me.* ²¹ *I went away full, but the Lord has brought me back empty. Why do you call me Naomi, since the Lord has testified against me and the Almighty has afflicted me?"*

²² *So Naomi returned, and with her Ruth the Moabitess, her daughter-in-law, who returned from the land of Moab. And they came to Bethlehem at the beginning of barley harvest.*

Introduction

It is said that if you can remember the seventies, you weren't there. I do remember a few things from the seventies, as I drifted in and out of a drug induced haze caused by my epilepsy medication. One of them was the attempt by Barry Benz, who is now the pastor of Gatton Church of Christ, to teach me how to preach. One thing I remember particularly clearly is Barry saying that you have to have a great introduction. You either win or lose your congregation in the first few sentences. I generally do not have too much trouble preparing a sermon. Reg[1] knows that as he has phoned me on a Saturday night and asked, "Ted, can you preach on Sunday?" "No problem, Reg." For months I have had a great introduction running around in my head, it started, "Is the Pope a Catholic?"

But we are being encouraged to listen to the "Whisper of God" and I was feeling a prompting to re-preach an old sermon. Its content seemed so appropriate to the situation some of us find ourselves in today. When Pastor Iain asked me to preach today much earlier than I expected due to Caroline's (his wife) surgery, I asked him, "What do you think?" However, my old friend Pastor Steer had told me that a re-preached sermon is like stale manna, great on the day, but stinks the day after. Still, I sent the sermon through to Iain and asked him his opinion. He said, "Ted, I think you are

---

1. A loved former elder.

right, half would not have been here, most would not remember, and I hope that those who do remember are full of Christian grace."[2]

Point 1. Why Ruth?

The advantage of being the preacher is that you get to preach from your favorite books and favorite passages, and Ruth is definitely my favorite book.[3] Why is it my favorite? Because it is not set in a royal palace, or a battlefield, or centered around a miracle worker, but in the day-to-day village life. Here there are no pillars of fire to lead a people that did not want to be led. God is in the shadows and men and women, young and old are publicly living the lives they should. It is a book in which everyone is certain that God will bless, but there is no mechanical connection between expectation and outcome. And to be honest, sometimes his blessings appear to come too late.

I decided it was time to read a good commentary and it didn't take long to realize what we have here, a small rural farming community, an old woman, a virtuous woman, a man of substance, a drought, foreign seasonal workers, an inheritance, a death of loved ones and, a Godlike bond between the players. Somewhere in this book is a message for Tenthill, and a message, I am bold enough to say, worth rehearing.

Point 2. What Is This Bond?

The bond is called *hesed*. In 2:20 we read, "He has not stopped showing his kindness, (*hesed*), to the living and the dead." Psalm 62:12 claims that *hesed* appears to be part of the very character of God because there we read, "To thee, oh Lord belongs steadfast love (*hesed*)." You see the same thing in Psalm 109:21, where God's *hesed* is good, or Psalm 63:3, God's *hesed* is better than life, and Psalm 136 where it lasts forever. One writer described it saying, "It is not a human achievement but a quality we know from God, a quality man is expected to emulate." In Ruth we see God's people at their best—showing *hesed*.

---

2. Only two people remembered.

3. This sermon would lead in time to a commentary on the book which has been published by Resource Publications, an imprint of Wipf and Stock.

Sermons from a Potato Field

	AV	RSV	NEB	GNB	NIV
Love words	-	182	149	162	171
Lovingkindness	30	-	-	-	1
Kindness words	43	29	4	19	49
Mercy words	155	2	-	-	7
Loyalty words	-	21	61	20	3
Promise	-	-	-	9	-
Devotion words	-	2	-	-	5
Favor	3	3	-	6	4
Goodness words	14	3	-	-	-
Miscellaneous	-	3	31	29	5

Table 1 Different Translations of Hesed

Hesed is a very difficult word to translate. In Ruth, we see it shown in a life of kindness above and beyond the call of duty. It is recommended and shown to be attainable. Are you kind? *Hesed* is achievable by Jew and Gentile. I want to talk more of this.

We know the great passage where Ruth declares her faith, "Your people will be my people and your God my God" but don't forget that either side is an expression of attachment of Ruth to her mother-in-law. This chapel is where you express your faith publicly; do you feel an attachment to those who gather here? This attachment is what makes the departure of those who went out painful.[4] Kindness overlooks so much and like love, covers a multitude of sins. Kindness won't let the bonds be broken, as much as it is in your power.

---

4. This was because of a disastrous pastorate.

Point 3. Ruth, a Virtuous Woman

To the young women, strive to be virtuous. Spiritual and virtuous are not the same. When I first spoke this message, I did not appreciate then how remarkable the young women in our church are, or how fortunate the young men are also. Boaz said to Ruth (3:11), "My people in the city know that you are a woman of excellence." On the way from Moab to Judah she says in 1:16, "Your people will be my people and your God my God." She arrives at the beginning of the barley harvest and by end of the wheat harvest the men of Bethlehem all know that Ruth is a virtuous woman. How much time has passed? You are the farmers. I am the "theologian,"[5] and I can tell you it's not enough for a deep work of sanctification.

She already possessed this virtue as a pagan. In 1:8 her mother-in-law said to her, "May the Lord show you kindness (*hesed*) to you as you have shown kindness (*hesed*) to your dead husbands and to me" (NIV). *Hesed*, here we have the word again, that word that is virtually untranslatable, perhaps loving kindness here. You can almost hear the bitter cry of Naomi, "Lord, you have deserted me, you have bought me nothing but misfortune where is your loving kindness? I look to you for it and find it only in my pagan daughters in law." Look at Ruth's love for her mother-in-law when she was a pagan. Look at her loyalty and diligence and determination, all when she was a pagan.

Some years back I went to Hungary to see a customer called Monica. I had seen her picture and I knew she was stunningly attractive. When I met her, I was only in her presence for a few minutes before I realized that there was something about her that I could only describe as "virtue." Her physical beauty was eclipsed by something that shone out from within her. Was she a Christian? I don't know, I don't think so. Our reading from Proverbs uses the same word as the one to describe Ruth. To have a noble character is wonderful.

Being virtuous is not the same thing as being spiritual and it is not the same as being good. Orpah, the other sister-in-law was good, she wasn't a failure, she was like God to Naomi because she also showed her *hesed* and Naomi was ready to bless her and commit her to God's care. Here in this little book virtue goes beyond being spiritual (which is difficult enough to define) and it goes beyond being good. Combine that with the fear of the

---

5. This refers to Sermon Four, *The Farmer and the Theologian*.

Lord and it is awesome. No wonder it is said to be rare. Yet I think we are blessed with that here in Tenthill.

How do you become virtuous? There is no Teach Yourself Book or Dummies Guide to being virtuous. The Good Lord is the only one who can teach you. Ask him.

Point 4. Boaz, a Man of Standing

Young men, you should strive to be like Boaz, a man of standing. A man of standing, what does it mean? Was he wealthy? He probably was. He has fields and workers and has enough money to purchase extra land. This is enough for men to call him a man of standing but not for God. He looks at his heart, not his wealth. He looks at his worth. Consider Boaz, he is so ready to bless. He blesses his workers, (2:4), and Ruth, (2:12, 3:10).

When I was visiting my friend Abeje in Addis Ababa in Ethiopia, we went for lunch one day with a friend of his. After the meal, this friend said to me, "Did you notice that I left a large tip?" He then went on to tell me a wonderful story. He told that when he was a young child, he helped financially three people including his uncle. I don't imagine it was a lot of money. His father heard about it, and said to him, "Kneel before me." He placed his hands on his head and asked our Lord to bless his son by always having money to give away. To that day, money comes to him from completely unexpected sources, and he keeps giving it away to people in need. My friends, do you bless people?

But it is not all words, Boaz blesses in deeds. He ensures that there is grain to glean. Ruth takes home eleven liters of grain. He commits Ruth to God's care and then does exactly what he wants God to do.

On that same trip to Ethiopia, we were travelling a country road when we were pulled over by a nun. She explained how a young lady had cut her hand and the injury needed stitches urgently so she could keep earning a living as a seamstress. She asked if we could take her to Addis Ababa? We agreed to take her as far as we were going. The nun said to her, "Go with God," but gave her no money as I expect she did not have any. As we came near to where we would part, I asked my friend. "She will have to pay for her surgery, won't she?" "Yes." "I don't imagine she has any money." "No." "What will it cost?" It was only a pittance, so I gave her twice that amount and extra for her bus fare home, then I committed her to God's grace. Prayers for God's deliverance are hypocritical when the answer is in your pocket all along.

Boaz treats people of low status with respect (2:13). He doesn't care what others think about him, (2:14-17). What did his workers think of this old man giving special favors to this young widow? He provides a safe workplace. "Stay in my field," he tells Ruth as in another person's field she might be hurt, (2:21-22). Not everybody in that small community lived as God would have them.

Then you have the curious events at the threshing floor. Even at my advanced age, if a young lady lay at my feet in the middle of the night it would have my attention. Would the outcome have been much different if Boaz had taken advantage of the situation? Probably not, but he does things properly. He doesn't rebuke her that night; he blesses her and says, "Don't let anyone see you."

Boaz is conscious of his responsibilities; he is the kinsman redeemer. Imagine that the best farm on the Long Lane[6] is going up for auction. The auctioneer stands up and spruiks the benefits of the property, but then adds that, as part of the deal, the successful bidder must marry the widow of the previous owner! It changes the dynamic of the auction somewhat. Boaz is a man who will not rest until important matters are settled. He goes beyond what is in his best interest (4:6).

You don't have to be rich to be a man of standing and being rich doesn't make you a man of standing. But it is very powerful when they do come together.

Point 5. What About the Drought?

There was a famine in the land, not just a drought. People were hungry. I remember my Ethiopian friend Abeje's comment that people in Australia do not go hungry when it doesn't rain. Elimelech, Naomi's husband was not much of a farmer as he hadn't learnt how to farm without water. But this wasn't Tenthill, this was the promised land, a land flowing with milk and honey. The conquest was fresh in the minds of the people. They knew about the Jordan parting, of Jericho's walls falling and of how the sun stood still. Boaz's mother was Rahab from Jericho. This is like my generation and the

---

6. The Lockyer Valley is one of the top ten most fertile areas in the world. The farms along the long straight road that connects Gatton, the main town for Tenthill are the most fertile in the area.

World War Two servicemen. They didn't see it happen, but they all knew the stories of God's mighty hand. They knew how God had bought mighty Egypt to its knees with his control of the weather, but in this land where I will show you *hesed*, why can't you make it rain?

It didn't rain on Boaz just as it didn't rain in Elimelech, Naomi's husband. One survived, the other didn't. We have no idea why. For one family it bought bitter reproach against God, (1:20–21). From the other it bought the blessing of God on those around them. Did Boaz have it easy? Famine had to have touched him also. Where is his wife, his family? But he did not come out of this twisted and wasn't angry with God. Yet I expect there were times that Boaz and his God had some frank words. Arguing with God is not always a sign of lack of faith, as one commentator says:

> Anyone who ascribes full sovereignty to a just and merciful God may expect to encounter the problem of theodicy, and to wrestle with that problem of sin, even when it leads to an attempt to put God on trial. Petulant Jonah, earnest Jeremiah, persistent Job, Naomi stands in their company.

But for Naomi, that had been eating at her for ten years.

Point 6. The Inheritance

This story climaxes around the inheritance, or the selling of it. Back six years ago I didn't know much about your affairs, I still do not know much but let me tell you about mine. For years it has been at risk–fire, an unpaid bill, a collapsed bridge[7]–with any of these there would be no or little inheritance. In the end two bad debts were enough for me to close my business and set me on a very uncertain path.

"What of yours?" I asked at the time I first preached this sermon, "What if the drought continues for another three years?" The weatherman said it was possible and I think it did. I remember laughing at the time in the Philippines when I heard an international weather report warning of an "increased danger of rain" for Queensland. If I stood here then and said it would be a flood that would really bring this valley low, you would have laughed at me.

The problem with inheritances is they are so uncertain. My Philippine friend Noe Galzote told me of the loss of inheritance because of

---

7. My company built many foot and road bridges.

preaching the gospel. He said to his daughter Joana, "All I can give you is an education." When my daughter was in high school, she pleaded for a pair of red tab Levi's that all the other girls were wearing. I was hard pressed financially at the time so I told her that while her friends might have red tab Levi jeans, she has got her daddy's genes, and that is far better. It kept her happy for a while.

Our children are not just our flesh and blood; they get far more from us. They learn their values, attitudes, and hopefully their spiritual beliefs. There is no greater inheritance we can receive than having a mother who is virtuous and a father who is a man of standing. No bank manager can ever repossess that. It can be squandered, just like the normal inheritance, but once the farm or the business has gone, it's gone. What you put into your children can be returned to at any time. "Return," it's the theme of chapter 1. The word occurs seventeen times.

Conclusion

Ruth has much to say to Tenthill. There are many sermons here, each of these points are worthy of a sermon in their own right and I have not done any of them justice, nor have I dealt with the old lady who can no longer work but can bless others with her words of advice and connections. Take from this what you need and remember we are all travelling well-trod paths. Over 3000 years have passed since Ruth went out to glean but the need to be exceptionally kind still remains, the need to be remarkable men and women remains. The need to trust him in today and for tomorrow still remains. And men and women can still be successful in living a God-fearing life.

Ruth was written during the time of the judges when all men did what was right in their own eyes. It was dark days for Israel and God's favor was regularly hidden. However, the Book of Ruth declared that not all men did what was right in their own eyes and that God is only hidden when we are the ones that hide him.

2

Eternity in Our Hearts

BACKGROUND: PASTOR IAIN WAS away on holidays and both I and the other relieving minister felt strongly that we needed to proclaim the gospel. A person who was new to the church was converted a few weeks later. Perhaps these messages had something to do with that, perhaps not.

Reading

Matthew 25:34–43, The parable of the sheep and goats.

Text: Philemon 12–20

12 *I have sent him back to you in person, that is, sending my very heart,* 13 *whom I wanted to keep with me, so that in your behalf he might be at my service in my imprisonment for the gospel;* 14 *but I did not want to do anything without your consent, so that your goodness would not be, in effect, by compulsion, but of your own free will.* 15 *For perhaps it was for this reason that he was separated from you for a while, that you would have him back forever,* 16 *no longer as a slave, but more than a slave, a beloved brother, especially to me, but how much more to you, both in the flesh and in the Lord.*

17 *If then you regard me as a partner, accept him as you would me.* 18 *But if he has wronged you in any way or owes you anything, charge that to my*

account; **19** *I, Paul, have written this with my own hand, I will repay it (not to mention to you that you owe to me even your own self as well).* **20** *Yes, brother, let me benefit from you in the Lord; refresh my heart in Christ.*

Point 1. What Is Your Soul Worth?

Eternity is written on our hearts[1]

For years, when I read through this portion of the New Testament I would rush over the little book of Philemon. Compare these few verses to the grandeur of Romans 8:

> **31** If God *is* for us, who *is* against us? **32** He who did not spare His own Son, but delivered Him over for us all, how will He not also with Him freely give us all things? **33** Who will bring charges against God's elect? God is the one who justifies; **34** who is the one who condemns? Christ Jesus is He who died, but rather, was raised, who is at the right hand of God, who also intercedes for us. **35** Who will separate us from the love of Christ?

What do you have? It's not even a book; it's just a letter, a private letter, about a runaway slave called Onesimus and a request to get the guest room ready. I suspect that for many here, you are much the same as me. Those great works of Paul that deal with eternity strike a chord with us because

---

1. Arthur Stace, known as Mr. Eternity, was an alcoholic from his teens until the early 1930's, when he converted to Christianity. He began to spread his message by inscribing the word "Eternity" with yellow chalk in copperplate writing on footpaths and doorsteps in and around Sydney, writing from Martin Place to Parramatta, from 1932 to his death in 1967. His one-word sermon is a legend in Sydney and his message and script was in lights on the Sydney Harbor Bridge for the millennium celebrations.

our Heavenly Father has written *eternity* in heart, yet the content of Philemon is so mundane, so every day (at least for those days), with not much relevance for today. How many of you own slaves? How could you compare it to Romans or Galatians? One ancient writer said of this letter, "The gospel is not concerned with trivia," because its focus is on this world. It is a book where we hear of love and of faith but there is none of the eternal hope, of that eternity written on our heart.

When our Lord returns, when those who are left meet him in the air, and those who were laid to rest in the sure and certain hope of the resurrection of dead are raised, we are told there is going to be a big party. I have said to the Lord, if he doesn't mind, I would like a slice of Joan Neuendorf's[2] lemon meringue pie. I suppose that would be quite literally, "Pie in the sky when you die." But this book deals with a very important question, and that is, is there (metaphorically speaking) any of Leone's sponge cake[3] or Sharon's rocky road in this world? Make no mistake; there wasn't any for the runaway slave Onesimus.

I wonder who is on morning tea wash up roster today. Who is on communion wash up this week? Whose turn is it to wash the feet of people coming to church this week? Mercifully for Barry and Graham[4] we don't do that. Who cleans the church, who attends every working bee? Back in the home church of Philemon it was a pretty short list. Every Sunday it was the same name in every position, the name Onesimus was in every slot. I am certain, that just as God has written eternity on our hearts, he has written freedom. And Onesimus wanted to be free.

This little book is more about the gospel than you may realize. In fact, it is all about the gospel. Paul wants Philemon to do him a favor, and it wasn't a small favor. We are told that an absolute drone of a slave cost 500 days wages. A skilled slave went for prices up to 100 times that. For this runaway slave to have been so valuable to Paul I don't imagine he was a drone. Can you imagine what is going through Philemon's mind? I suspect it was something like, "Paul, do you know what you are asking? Do you know how much he cost? I'll just give him a severe flogging and we will say no more of it." Then, while on the subject of money and punishment for sin, Paul says to Philemon, "You owe me your very self." "You owe me your

---

2. Joan is a wonderful cook as you probably gathered.

3. I told Leone that her sponge cakes should come with a health warning as there must be nail holding them down on the plate as they are so light. Sharon's rocky road is just superb.

4. Our greeters at the door.

very self." Membership of Christ's church is not like membership of Rotary or a debating society, or a gardening club or whatever it is that takes your fancy. We don't like to talk about Hell any longer, but Jesus did, and Paul did. There is eternal life and there is eternal death and Paul's ministry had bought Philemon from death to life. He owed Paul, his very self, there is no greater debt you can owe a man.

What is your eternal soul worth Philemon? Is it worth as much as your slave, is it worth as much as the estimated 5–6,000,000 slaves in the Roman empire? Is it worth as much as the Roman empire itself? Jesus said that if you gain all this and lose your soul it profits you nothing. The God of this universe died on a cross so we can be free from sin and from Hell and that makes it worth more than all these. The God of this universe wants you to live with him forever. You neglect your soul to your eternal peril.

Point 2. Christ Makes the Useless Useful

Sometimes my name is more than I can bear

Have you ever considered how well brother Greg[5] was named? I have known him for many years, long before he became a Baptist. I was always impressed at how astute he was in his dealings. You would have to say he was sharp in the best sense of the word. When Anne took him home to meet her parents, I am sure they would have to have thought, "Our daughter is blessed, here is a young man, not just Sharpe in name but sharp and vigilant in all he does." (Gregory means vigilant.) I am sad to say there was nothing so illustrious for me. I am afraid I was called Teddy when I was young. As I got older it was more than I could bear. Even recently at Sorellas,[6] it was Teddy! But I

---

5. Greg Sharpe was an elder in the church. He is also an astute businessman.

6. My favourite coffee shop. It is situated in Forest Hill, Queensland and worth going out of your way to find.

suspect Rachel[7] in her weaker moments, and if no one is looking, would occasionally like to cuddle me. There are names that hint at great promise, and some less so. Things have not changed over the millennia.

Just imagine, Philemon wants to purchase his wife a new multi-function labor saving device for the home, but far more functional than a Thermomix. It will do all that machine will do and also be a dishwasher, vacuum cleaner and food preparation unit and dog walker all in one. Yes, he is going to purchase a slave, just like buying a tractor, or a cow! Slave traders and used chariot salesmen the world over were tarred with the same brush. You can almost hear him say to Philemon, "Here we have a real bargain, his name is "useful" (for that is what Onesimus means) and he will be useful to your wife as he is hardworking, honest, conscientious, subservient, run on the smell of an oily rag, only driven on Sunday by an old lady. He is well named, and he is on special today."

Well, Philemon purchased a lemon! Onesimus really should have been called "useless" or" unprofitable." The promise conjured up with his name failed to materialize. It appears that the situation was so unbearable for Onesimus that he put his hand in the till and cleared off halfway across the empire to escape his affectionate master (that is what Philemon means.) Perhaps they were glad to see the back of him. Perhaps Philemon wasn't such an affectionate master! When I was twenty years old, I went for a six-month adventure across half the world. I did not know that the hound of heaven would pursue me down my "labyrinthine ways," in Ceylon, Kenya and London I was confronted by a God who was real and who wanted me to know him, just like he knew me. Here I was, a church attendee for twenty years but was never a child of God. What of you, young people, has Christ captured you heart. He wants you to know him and to trust him whatever life brings your way.

What are the chances of a runaway slave from Turkey running away to find anonymity in Rome and coming across Paul, a friend of his master? This was not chance and there is no chance in your life. God's grace and his mercy were poured upon you from your birth and indeed right from your very conception. But to have your footsteps guided by your maker as you walk alone is not the same thing as having new life. The journey is not the destination. Your Father's love and his care for you in your childhood and youth was so you may know him and walk beside him forever. "He loves me" you might say, but our Heavenly Father loves the image of his son that

---

7. My long-suffering wife.

Eternity in Our Hearts

he will create in you far more. And he did that in a useless runaway slave, what of you? Young people, before you know it, you will be sixty, seventy, even eighty and you will be wondering where the years have gone. Are you going to walk those years alone?

When Paul sent Onesimus back, he wrote to Philemon in verse 11 saying, "Formerly he was useless to you, but now he has become useful both to you and to me." I love word plays and here we have a beauty, and it would not have been lost on Philemon as there was nothing subtle about it. It would have been like hitting him between the eyes with a piece of 4x2. His useless slave called "useful" now actually was "useful," and that is pretty clever pun on his name. That is what Jesus does when he comes into a life, he makes bad people good, and he makes good people better.

Paul's wordplay is far deeper and, as I said, not very subtle. He puts the end of any thought of flogging the runaway slave. He does not use forms of the word "Onesimus" which you would expect, but he uses a different word for useful, "*chrestos,*" a word the scholars tell us is pronounced exactly the same as *christos* (our Christ.) We know the Romans mixed these two words up. In those days you never read quietly in your mind but out aloud. You heard what you read. Here Philemon would in effect hear Paul say, "He left you without Christ and is returning with Christ." Now word plays don't come more profound than that. Paul said in Galatians 3:28, "There is neither Jew nor Gentile, neither slave nor free, nor is there male and female . . . ," but there is with Christ and without Christ

Listen to what Paul says to the slave owner, "17 So if you consider me a partner, welcome him as you would welcome me. 18 But if he has wronged you in any way or owes *you anything*, charge that to my account; 19 I, Paul, have written *this* with my own hand, I will repay *it.*" Luther's commentary says, "Here we see how St. Paul lays himself out for poor Onesimus, and with all his means pleads his cause with his master: and so, sets himself as if he were Onesimus, and had himself done wrong to Philemon. Even as Christ did for us with God the father, thus also St. Paul does for Onesimus with Philemon . . . we are all his Onesimi, to my thinking." Jesus says to your Heavenly Father for you, "Put it to my account I will repay," for no one else could. Would that I was an evangelist, Matt French a few weeks ago believed strongly that he had to proclaim the gospel and he did it powerfully.

For months now, I have felt the Lord laying on my heart to share with you the words, "You owe me your life." Is there one here who is struggling to make that leap into the unknown? Is there someone here who struggles with the life of faith? Imagine a promissory note on the Bank of Rangoon in Indian rupees, what foolish things people have trusted in. The promissory note our Savior offers you is a guarantee that has been written out in the blood of Jesus. Father, put that person's sin to my account, I will repay.

Point 3. Saved to Serve

A while back, I met for coffee with my old friend Eric Liebelt[8]. When we discussed today's sermon he got talking about the great "Lutheran heresy"—they are his words not mine. That "heresy" he said was thinking it is enough to be saved and then sit in the pews for the rest of your life. Many of us have been blessed by the vision of that church when he was pastor; my own family has been particularly blessed. As you know he retired and went to Mount Barker. He has just built a $2m accommodation center for the disabled in that town which, incidentally, is run by the Baptists. That is despite stronger opposition in that town from their council than ever he had from Gatton council. It is totally debt free. Now at seventy-eight he is wondering, what the Lord has got for him to do now. Getting saved is not like crossing something off your bucket list, what is next, cruise the Nile and see the pyramids? No!! It is something that you live and drives you to the day you die.

A local reporter asked Eric on the thirtieth anniversary of Peace school, "Why did you do all this" and he replied, "Are you a Christian?" "Yes." "Then you should not have to ask that question." And I shouldn't need a third point to this sermon which I have called, "You are saved to serve." You were not called to a faith without deeds for such a faith would be dead and pointless. Look at Philemon. He did not say to those around him, "Go in peace, be warmed and be filled," but do nothing about their physical needs, what good is such a faith? He did not say, "Things might be pretty grim for you but don't forget you have a hope in heaven." Paul knew how he met those needs with faith and love. He said, "For I have had great joy and comfort in your love, because the hearts of the saints have been refreshed through you, brother."

---

8. Eric was the former pastor of Peace Lutheran Church, Gatton and a mentor and close friend to me. During his ten-year pastorate, the church was actively involved in establishing a primary and secondary school, services to the disabled and much expanded facilities for the aged. Interestingly the local council fought it every inch of the way.

Eternity in Our Hearts

Why is it a great heresy to say that you are saved just to sit on seats? Because God's word that says you are saved by grace also says the words in Matthew 25 that were read out this morning, "⁴¹ "Then He will also say to those on His left, 'Depart from Me, you accursed people, into the eternal fire which has been prepared for the devil and his angels; ⁴² for I was hungry, and you gave Me nothing to eat; I was thirsty, and you gave Me nothing to drink; ⁴³ I was a stranger, and you did not invite Me in; naked, and you did not clothe Me; sick, and in prison, and you did not visit Me.'" (And I would have to be the worst visitor in the church.)

Wooh, Ted, are you saying faith in Jesus is not enough? What I am saying is that we do not have enough of Jesus. Look at what Paul said to Philemon in verse six, "I pray that your partnership with us in the faith may be effective in deepening your understanding of every good thing we share for the sake of Christ." Paul is asking a generous man to be even more generous. What Paul appears to be saying to this man that had refreshed so many people was that you learn about Christ by giving to others. By emptying ourselves we are filled with Christ. You do not learn about Jesus through scholarship, (and I am not saying anything against growth through study, I have done my fair share) nor through days of prayer, (and I am not minimizing the importance of prayer, and I have not done my fair share.) Ultimately, we learn it through loving generosity towards our fellow men, the Christ we can see, our friends, our employees, and strangers.

Conclusion

George Whitfield was probably the greatest evangelist of the eighteenth century. His voice was so powerful that 25,000 people are recorded as hearing him at once, and yet, so musical and well-toned that someone said, "He could raise tears by his pronunciation of the word 'Mesopotamia.'" Lord, today I needed that eloquence, but I am not an orator. If you could hear the passion behind my Pilipino friend Noe Galzote when he preaches the gospel your heart would melt, and faith would come easily. Lord, I needed some of that passion today. If you could see my mad⁹ American mate Fred Kornis just stop in the street of a third world country and start doing rope tricks and people gather around him as he uses those tricks to explain the gospel, faith would rise up in you. But Lord I am too timid when I try to share your gospel. This morning you have the message of eternity and

---

9. In the nicest sense of the word.

you only have me to communicate it. One day I will figure out what gifts and calling God has given me, but I know it is not evangelism. I am not eloquent, and I lack the passion needed to stress upon you how urgent this matter is.

In my life I have heard some memorable sounds; sounds that I expect will ring in my ear to the day I die, As I walked up from the town of Capel in Surrey UK to the Bible College in 1974, I heard a sound that will be with me to the day I die. It was the sound of a 1928 Bentley blower. It had a monster four-cylinder engine with a supercharger bolted on. Or in 1970 when I was travelling the Norfolk Broads in England and was buzzed by a flight of spitfires with their twelve-cylinder supercharged Rolls Royce Merlin engines. But there is one sound that is far more precious than all of these, a sound you will never forget, and that is the sound of the gospel being preached when you first believed. That glorious day, when you renounced the enemy of your soul and grasped firmly the eternal light and life of our loving Savior. The day you decided not to walk alone. You will remember the date and the place, and it will be forever precious. Is today that day for you?

I would dare say to you all, to whom do you owe your very life? I owe it to a brother of Jack xxxx,[10] a man who was into every manner of depravity before he stopped in his tracks by God's salvation, so do not tell me there isn't a gracious God, who saves the unexpected-by-unexpected means. Don't leave this place until you make your Heavenly Father your friend. Talk to me, talk to an elder, talk to your friends, it is a path well-trodden in this church. Many have gone before you. Today start the supercharged adventure of a lifetime, a lifetime that encompasses eternity.

---

10. A local and somewhat likable rogue. He has been baptised four times on last count I believe.

3

The Dark Night of the Soul

Setting

READER, I HOPE YOU never have to understand what is written in this sermon. It came from the deepest despair of my soul when my wife was given up for dead with cancer (and before the Lord intervened.)

Text: Hebrews 11:17–19.

7 By faith Abraham, when he was tested, offered up Isaac, and the one who had received the promises was offering up his only son; **18** *it was he to whom it was said, "Through Isaac your descendants shall be named."* **19** *He considered that God is able to raise people even from the dead, from which he also received him back as a type.*

At the last men's fellowship, Pastor Iain asked me if I would swap preaching dates with Phil[1] because of his workload. "Not a problem" which is shorthand for, "What are you thinking about? I am preaching in Nowra, I have to prepare a Gideon address for re-accreditation, make some progress on

---

1. Phil was completing his final year at the Baptist training college in Brisbane.

my next essay for the UK course and prepare a sermon on top of this!!!" A couple of days later, Pastor Iain rang and asked me if I would speak on Hebrews 11:17–19, Abraham sacrificing Isaac. I thought, "Here is another proof that there is a merciful God!" When I was a much younger man, I had written an exposition of the life of Isaac from the Hebrew text, I knew the story well, this was going to be easy. As I meditated on the story, I wished that Pastor Iain had given me some other passage as I would never bring you this sermon by choice. The story of the sacrifice is not just an hour or so on Mount Moriah. We can easily forget it is a story that covers a three-day trial of faith on the journey from the wells of Beersheba to Moriah.

Young people, much of what I am going to say you will have no concept of. Thank God for that. I ask you to bury these words deep in your heart for when you are old. Then some of you may well say, "Now I understand what old Ted was talking about."

Abraham had been tested many times. Sometimes he passed with flying colors and sometimes he failed dismally, but overall, his life was an amazing success and God had acknowledged this. Seven chapters earlier we read:

> **4** Then behold, the word of the Lord came to him, saying, "This man will not be your heir; but one who will come from your own body shall be your heir." **5** And He took him outside and said, "Now look toward the heavens and count the stars, if you are able to count them." And He said to him, "So shall your descendants be." **6** Then he believed in the Lord; and He credited it to him as righteousness.

When he was still called Abram, he believed God's promise about the future birth of his son Isaac and God, for his part, imputed righteousness to him. The debit side of the slate was wiped clean, paid in full by his greatest descendant. This was never a self-righteousness where Abraham had to pass every test to maintain his position of friendship with God. The righteousness given to him by God was big enough to accommodate failure, and he would still fail. Remember the faith that has been given to you is big enough to cover your failures as well.

The Dark Night of the Soul

Australian light horse memorial at Beersheba

Abraham was now at ease, even though he did not own a square inch of the land promised to him, but God had given him his promised son. Despite his land being marginal at best, he now lived at peace with his neighbors, and he had guaranteed access to enough water. Ninety years ago, last week, the 4th and 12th Australian Light Horse charged across the deserts of Beersheba in a do or die effort to gain access to Abraham's well. All that was left for Abraham was to see out his days in peace and be buried by his son and not his servant.

In his ease, Satan's taunt about Job could equally be applied to Abraham as in this modified version of Job 1:9–11:

> 9 Then Satan answered the Lord, "Does [Abraham] fear God for nothing? 10 Have You not made a fence around him and his house and all that he has, on every side? You have blessed the work of his hands, and his possessions have increased in the land. 11 But reach out with Your hand now and touch all that he has; he will certainly curse You to Your face."

One night *the God,* spoke to him, an unusual expression. There was no doubt who was talking, and said to old Abraham, "Take your son, your only son, Isaac, the one that you love (and there was no doubt about who he was talking about), and sacrifice and burn his body at a place I will show you." This is not the language of dreams, the senility of old age or Satan appearing as an angel of light. The impulses of faith had crossed over to hard reality of the circumstances of life. The idols of stone of Ur of the Chaldees where he grew up needed sacrifices, so they did not go hungry, but even they did not require this of their worshipers. But the living God who needs nothing comes to Abraham and says, "Give to me that which is most precious to you. Give to me all that you have strived for in the past, give to me your hopes for your future."

God's command to Abraham is totally incomprehensible. The German commentator Von Rad said, "This narrative concerns something more frightful than child sacrifice. It has to do with a road out into God forsakenness, a road on which Abraham does not know that God is only testing him." This command Calvin called, "the destruction of faith." This was not, to quote Calvin again, "the dispensations of his providence which often appear in contradiction to his word." These dispensations were trials he had already passed in relation to the promise of his long-awaited son, these trials are common to the saints. I pray God that none ever know the depth of this testing we read of here, but many have. It is common enough for it to have a name, *the Dark Night of the Soul.* The expression comes from a work by St John of the Cross, a sixteenth century Carmelite priest. Recently it has been revealed that Mother Teresa of Calcutta experienced this from 1946 to her death in 1997 apart from a few interludes. The old church fathers knew of it also under the name of *Dues Absconditus,* the God who hides himself.

You will probably say back to me, "Ted, look around you, this is not Calcutta; there are no statues or crucifix here. This is an evangelical Baptist church in twenty-first century rural Queensland. We know nothing of an experience of loneliness and desolation in our spiritual lives. I have a strong prayer life and my devotion to God has been long and constant. I can never imagine that I could suddenly find prayer extremely difficult and unrewarding for an extended period of time. I could never imagine that I could feel suddenly abandoned." But perhaps there are one or two of you here who have had to deal with what Calvin called the "dispensations of his providence," that know exactly what I am saying. During my wife's cancer battle in 1988, I personally knew such a time.

The Dark Night of the Soul

The three days travelling to Moriah were a time in which Abraham would travel with his son, eat with him, talk with him, even sleep with the young boy huddled up next to his bosom. As the old church father Origen wrote, he would have to "confront, in the course of the journey, the paternal feelings and his faith, the love of God and the love of the flesh, the attraction of the things of the present and the expectation of things to come." We may not comprehend what a spectacle the stars were in those clear desert nights, as he looked to the heavens. Every one of those stars was meant to represent one of his descendants through Isaac. As he looked at the promise in the stars how could he reconcile the sacrifice? Many times, Abraham would have seen the smoke rise from the high places as another father sacrificed his son, but he did not worship the vicious and cruel god of the Canaanites.

Over three days, what did he think about? Did he ask, "Has God overnight changed his nature and his plans for me?" Did Abraham question whether he had committed some grievous sin? Did he ask, "Was the friendship broken?" These were the questions faith had to answer. But did Abraham remember that in the face of the impossible, the Lord had delivered Sarah and himself on many occasions. Did he think about God's faithfulness and care over a long life? Did he contemplate whether God was as good as his promises? Was the multitude of descendants through Isaac a core or a non-core promise?[2] Did he think about the difference between his God, the God who revealed himself as God Almighty and the vicious Gods of Canaan? Abraham's God had only asked that he walk before him and be holy, the Canaanite gods demanded more than a man could bear to give. Did he remember how when he was a young man, God told him to leave his home and family in Mesopotamia to a place he did not know, just like now, and how the guide of his soul had had a true and certain map for his future?

Sometime in those three days of despair Abraham came to the conclusion that, despite his outward circumstances, God was fully trustworthy. Abraham had worked through his own dark night of his soul. He had set out with a command from God to sacrifice his son but by the time he reached Moriah he said to his servants, "I and the boy will go over there; and we will worship and return to you." Abraham didn't know exactly what was before him, but he did know that whatever it was it did not have to be feared and if God had to raise Isaac from the dead, he would do just that. Just as he will

---

2. This refers to pledges made at election time by Australian political parties where they distinguish what they will promise to do and what they would like to do.

do it to you and me. As one old commentator said, "He bought his reason into captivity to the obedience of faith."

What happened then on that mount is a mystery. According to Josephus, Isaac is twenty-five years old at the time of the sacrifice, while the Jewish sages taught that Isaac is thirty-seven. Isaac, a young strong youth allows an old man of over 120 to tie him. Isaac probably had to help Abraham get him on the altar. This test of faith was as much for Isaac as it was for Abraham. Later chapters will not have a great deal to say about Isaac and what is said could leave us with the impression that he was second rate when compared with his father, but this sacrifice will show him to be giant of faith with confidence in his God who asked for the unspeakable and confidence in his father whom he let bind him. Difference to our parents does not mean inferior.

Why do the trials of our faith come? One commentator said he was in danger of loving something more than loving God. But if God was to judge our temptations who could stand? The reason the Angel of the Lord gave was, "Now I know that you fear God," but that doesn't help. God Almighty already knows the deepest secrets of our hearts. He knows if we fear him or not. The trials of our faith are never to show God that we are worthy of his favor because we never were and never will be. Perhaps there is some merit in rephrasing the angles words, "Now Abraham *you* know that you fear God."

This was not a case of divine brinkmanship; the ram was prepared and caught by its horns in the thicket. It was just hidden from their view just as the God that Abraham thought he knew, and did know, was hidden from his view. The culmination of the story is all about God seeing Abraham and Isaac. The fire and the wood are here, Isaac said, "But where is the lamb for the burnt offering." Abraham replied, "The Lord will provide (see) for himself." Afterwards Abraham called the place Jehovah-Jireh, "The Lord he sees," and Moriah itself probably means, "The manifestation of Jehovah." Yes, at times we might lose sight of our loving Savior, but our reason can be bought into the obedience of faith and can take hold of the true and certain knowledge that our Lord sees us and in his seeing is our ultimate provision.

The twelfth century rabbi, Rashi, commenting on Jeremiah 7:31 stated: "Tophet is Moloch, which was made of brass; and they heated him from his lower parts; and his hands being stretched out, and made hot, they put the child between his hands, and it was burnt; it vehemently cried out; but the priests beat a drum, that the father might not hear the voice of his

The Dark Night of the Soul

son, and his heart might not be moved." That passage in Jeremiah which he is referring to says, "And they go on building the high place of Topheth, which is in the valley of the son of Hinnom, to burn their sons and their daughters in the fire—which I did not command, nor did it come into my mind." What has come into the mind of God Almighty concerning you? In Jeremiah 29 we read, "[11] 'For I know the plans that I have for you,' declares the Lord, 'plans for prosperity and not for disaster, to give you a future and a hope. [12] Then you will call upon Me and come and pray to Me, and I will listen to you. [13] And you will seek Me and find *Me* when you search for Me with all your heart. [14] I will let Myself be found by you,' declares the Lord, 'and I will restore your fortunes...'"

How sweet were the Almighty's promises to Abraham? Afterwards, no longer would he picture his descendants like the hot dry sands of the deserts he had trudged for a century. They would be like the sand on the seashore, white and clean, washed daily by the oceans with its salt that preserves and flavors.

4

The Farmer and the Theologian

Background

THIS SERMON WAS PREACHED in 2006. Out Church had received help from a larger church and now we were in a position to help another smaller church. I had been involved with supporting third world pastors for some time and had found it a great blessing to those helped and to me. I put out the challenge to the church to support an Indian pastor. This was taken up a couple of years later.

Text: Acts 15:36-39.

6 After some days Paul said to Barnabas, "Let's return and visit the brothers and sisters in every city in which we proclaimed the word of the Lord, and see how they are." 37 Barnabas wanted to take John, called Mark, along with them also. 38 But Paul was of the opinion that they should not take along with them this man who had deserted them in Pamphylia and had not gone with them to the work. 39 Now it turned into such a sharp disagreement that they separated from one another, and Barnabas took Mark with him and sailed away to Cyprus.

The Farmer and the Theologian

How often have you heard the challenge to be more like Jesus? There is no higher goal, but what I am setting before you is the challenge to be more like the Holy Spirit. Well Ted, I don't think I have heard that before, you have to be skating on thin ice! Where is your proof text? Well, we will get to it. But first let me remind you of some old history

Paul and Barnabas were arguing about John Mark who had deserted them on the first missionary journey. What do we know about John Mark who is usually known as just Mark? He was a relative of Barnabas and most likely lived in Jerusalem. After Paul and Barnabas brought the offering from Antioch to drought affected Jerusalem, Mark travelled back to Antioch with them. You would reasonably expect that he ministered with Paul and Barnabas at some level before accompanying them on the missionary journey.

On that journey, something happened in Crete. Up to that time it had always been Barnabas and Saul and thereafter it would be Paul and Barnabas. After the team left Cyprus and arrived in Paphos in Pamphylia, John Mark deserted the team. Suggestions for why he left are numerous, here are just four:

1. He was put out by his uncle being demoted,
2. He got cold feet when the dangers of preaching to a hostile audience, the risk of disease, or physical rigors came home to him,
3. John Chrysostom, the golden mouthed preacher, says it was because he wanted his mother, and
4. He lacked conviction.

Whatever the reason, Paul considered it desertion!!

What do we know about Barnabas? This is where we get to our proof text in Acts 4, **36** "Joseph, a Levite from Cyprus, whom the apostles called Barnabas (which means son of encouragement), **37** sold a field he owned and brought the money and put it at the apostles' feet."

Barnabas was called the *Son of Encouragement* or *consolation*, (*paráklēsis*). You don't have to be a Greek scholar to recognize the word. Jesus was the *Consolation of Israel*, the same word, and he promised that on his departure He would send us another comforter just like him, the *paráklētos*, the Holy Spirit.

We read in Acts 11:24 that Barnabas was a good man, full of the Holy Spirit. This filling of the Holy Spirit led to great acts of compassion, so much so that that he sold excess property to alleviate the poverty of the Jerusalem church. His generosity of heart shaped the New Testament church. Consider what Barnabas has done up to this heated argument with Paul:

1. It was Barnabas who was sent to Antioch when the gospel was being preached to Gentiles for the first time. He sent a favorable reply and stayed to minister. Where would we have been if another man was sent?
2. He was able to convince the Jerusalem church that Saul the persecutor was soundly converted and was now an ally,
3. He left a thriving ministry in Antioch to personally seek out Saul in Tarsus to help in Antioch when he had been sidelined through mistrust,
4. It was he, along with Saul, who sent an offering from Antioch to Jerusalem when there was a drought,
5. It was he who, along with Saul, was called by the Spirit for the first missionary journey, and
6. It was he who was more God like than Paul. In Lystra where Paul healed a lame person, the Greeks wanted to worship them. Paul, they called Hermes as he did all the talking but Barnabas they called Zeus, the head of the gods.

Such was his bearing and nature. I can think of only a few people I have known that had/have such greatness of spirit. If that isn't being like the Holy Spirit, I don't know what is. And now he wants to take the quitter Mark and entrust him again with the spreading of the gospel. Paul had forgotten the soundness of this man's judgement and the size of his heart. Barnabas didn't bow down to Paul and he took John Mark and left Paul. In Barnabas' mind, Paul was the dispensable one, not Mark. Barnabas was saying in effect, Paul, you are concerned about the ministry, but I am concerned about the minister.

Who was right the farmer or the theologian? Barnabas realized God wasn't finished with Mark despite his failure/s. This quitter is accredited by church tradition as founding the church at Alexandria, the third city of the empire. Later he would emerge as a servant of Paul in Rome as a most useful servant (2 Tim 4:11), a man most wanted by Paul at the end. Peter would describe him as, "Mark my son" (1 Pet. 5:8). Papias an early church historian said of the gospel he was eventually to write, "Mark who was Peter's interpreter, wrote down accurately, though not in order all that he recollected of what Christ had said or done." This man could have been

The Farmer and the Theologian

easily lost to the church; and we owe his "redemption" to Barnabas whose big heart was again to change the history of the church. Barnabas' greatness was possibly not in what he did for God, but what he made possible for others to do, including Paul, the Antioch church and John Mark. If this is not Spirit like I do not know what is.

Can we do it too? Let me digress and share from my heart. We have started the involved process of calling a pastor. Last Sunday we started hearing how difficult that might be. One minister's condition was that his children only attend a certain high school. If we could pack up Tenthill and move it within a half hour drive of the coast, there would be no problem. But we can't do that and why should we?

Standing at the back door of the manse looking over the valley would have to be the closest thing to heaven this side of glory. Do we ever think how easy our service for Christ is compared to others? Let me tell you about my friend Noe, a Pilipino pastor and you will never doubt it. I first met Noe a little over ten years ago. I was speaking at a conference he had organized in General Santos City in Southern Mindanao, the bombing capital of the Philippines. It was organized to train tribal pastors. Noe, who was then the principal of a Bible college in Manila, told me how one day he visited one of these tribal churches. It was no more than a thatched roof on four posts. The pastor was preaching his heart out when a strong wind came up and blew away the pages of his tattered paperback Bible. He had to leave everything to run after the pages before they were lost.

That day the Lord touched Noe's heart and he decided then and there that he would do whatever he could to serve these men and their families. For the love of Christ, they would go where no one else would go. No training—trained men seldom wanted to go back to the bush, no education for their children, no healthcare, no financial support. The head of the mission said, "These men and their wives serve faithfully for many years in these conditions and all they ask for is vitamins."

One of these men walked five hours just to get to the road to come to the conference. The head of the mission asked the speakers, "Would we help this man?" He was a former guerrilla, and he has the opportunity to have Bible studies with them but can only do it at night. "Can we help him with a pressure lamp?" The few dollars it cost was the churches total offering for nine months!

A couple of days later Noe spoke at a gospel meeting where he was interpreting for an American evangelist. I have never heard or felt the gospel preached with such intensity, not from the evangelist, and he was no slouch, but through the translation. Noe had a fire in his belly, the fire I knew I should have had but didn't and still don't. Lord, forgive me. I thought, what could this man do if he was empowered financially? I decided there and then that here was a man that deserved and needed my help. And right away I started to go through a time when we were very hard pressed financially. We barely had two shillings to rub together.

He didn't write to me saying, "Ted, my children are hungry; my wife is having a breakdown because of the bombs and the poverty." Our friendship grew though; it wasn't based on money but on a bond that comes with likeminded people.

I went back to see him perhaps five years ago. He had returned to Manila with his tail between his legs, bruised and financially ruined. He had sold his inheritance, culturally a big issue for him, and built a six-meter by six-meter home above his father-in-law's shop, squatting on government land in a floodway in a Manila slum. I had just paid off my big home and I saw my friend, a far better man than I, living like that and it cut me to the quick. I made a promise to give more assistance and by God's grace we have. This man, who many would say his ministry failed, was picked up by our Lord, dusted down and given a ministry back again. He was at the time the superintendent of a group of over 150 churches. The Lord let Rachel and I be a part of that.

Does your heart burn with gospel? I don't mean do you love Jesus, I know you do, but do you burn with passion to see the lost saved? I am not going to say "why not" because I would have to condemn myself. But I can say, "If it doesn't burn with fire, empower someone who does have the fire." Money is short you might say, we have all either been there or are there. Believe me, it generally passes. What does it cost to befriend someone? To know him by name, to know his wife and children by name, to pray for them, to share in their joys and sorrows

Fred Astaire was once an aspiring entertainer and along came that day that all budding actors long for, his first screen test. Most of you youngsters are looking at me blankly, who was Fred Astaire? Well, he gave my father's generation a lot of pleasure and I still enjoy a Fred Astaire film. That day came and went. What was the result? "Can't sing, can't act, can dance a little." But someone in the studio had the financial sense to invest in him. You know what he needed? A good partner and the studio found him one,

The Farmer and the Theologian

Ginger Rogers. It is said that she did everything Fred Astaire did but backwards and in high heels.

My simple challenge to you today is to invest in someone, partner with someone, someone who will bring more than just fleeting pleasure to others but eternal life. Everybody loves a winner, someone that has a past written for everyone to read. It not so easy to back someone that just has a future known only to God. How do you find someone if you do not have contacts? It is not hard. In this whole sorry world where should I seek a partner and I suggest India. Why India, why not India is more the point. Nearly one in three in India lives in absolute poverty. There is also a significant difference between the levels of development of the rural and urban areas. How dreadful the plight must be for many ministers of the gospel who live in country areas.

But Ted, I am already giving to the church, I heard the last financial report, there isn't money to spare in the church budget. I am not saying "Instead of," but, "As well as." Some will say my budget is already tight, too tight to partner with someone. How much does it cost anyway? Well let's start at something achievable. My weakness is coffee. We all have something. A coffee costs $3.50, and a coffee and New York cheesecake is $7.50. So, if we make a really big sacrifice and drop one coffee a week, we have almost $200 in a year. If we give up the cake, we have $350. Literally, the crumbs off our table.

What can you do? Ted, are you saying, "Invest in the ministry? Underwrite an evangelistic campaign?" No!! I am saying invest in the minister:

- Pay for a family to build a hygienic toilet,
- Pay the school costs for educating their children—40 percent are illiterate,
- Pay the wedding for one of the daughters, even
- Allow them to have a holiday.

You know, this is so easy today, global money transfers with Western Union, email, (in the back blocks of Ethiopia when I was there recently, internet cafés existed) and if all else fails there is still snail mail. As the relationship grows from duty (for lack of a better word) to friendship to family you will be amazed how the Lord will empower you financially. Noe's daughter is no longer the hungry girl doubting the goodness of God but a very godly young woman in the final stages of university. What a return on our investment. You will be amazed with your investment. You will be amazed where the money comes from.

Do this and you also will be like Barnabas, the son of consolation, and you will be like the Holy Spirit to them. Great will be your reward in heaven and on that great day you will find that your love will have covered a multitude of sins.

5

On Appointing a New Pastor

Background

OUR CHURCH WENT THROUGH a devastating time following the appointment of a pastor that saw the congregation's numbers halve. The church then went through an "Intentional Interim Ministry" under Alan and Rosemary Gordon. I joined the church during his ministry. They have become close friends. Over Alan's two-year period he guided the church through the healing process and the calling of a new pastor. Appointing a new pastor has always been a troubling time as I have been unfortunate to have experienced some pastors that have troubled rather than blessed the church. The sermon was preached in 2007 before the members meeting where a decision had to be made whether to extend a call to our next pastor.

Text: Revelation 2:1–7

"To the angel of the church in Ephesus write:
The One who holds the seven stars in His right hand, the One who walks among the seven golden lampstands, says this:
2 'I know your deeds and your labor and perseverance, and that you cannot tolerate evil people, and you have put those who call themselves apostles to the test, and they are not, and you found them to be false; 3 and

you have perseverance and have endured on account of My name, and have not become weary. **4** *But I have this against you, that you have left your first love.* **5** *Therefore, remember from where you have fallen, and repent, and do the deeds you did at first; or else I am coming to you and I will remove your lampstand from its place—unless you repent.* **6** *But you have this, that you hate the deeds of the Nicolaitans, which I also hate.* **7** *The one who has an ear, let him hear what the Spirit says to the churches. To the one who overcomes, I will grant to eat from the tree of life, which is in the Paradise of God.'*

We are going to vote on a new pastor. The easiest thing to do when preparing this sermon is to ignore it and preach about something simple and without any controversy. But to be allowed the pulpit is both a privilege and a responsibility and the speaker must be careful not to abuse that privilege or fail in the responsibility.

A couple of weeks ago when we first looked at calling a new minister, I was sitting in this building with a knot in my stomach wishing I was an Anglican or a Methodist. Why, because the bishop or the moderator in Brisbane will choose the man and send him to us, and we would have little or no say about who that man is. If it all goes wrong, we can blame the bishop. But we cannot do that, we are Baptists. We appointed a search committee to look for us using guidelines we as a membership gave them. If the new pastor is a great success and our church grows and prospers there can be pats all around for the search committee. What a wonderful job they did. If not, if the church doesn't prosper, we can't blame the committee because we as a congregation made our choice and buck stops with us, and no one else.

But why was my stomach in a knot? Because years ago, I was on a committee, and I did not explore the unease and disquiet in my heart and recommended a man to the church who destroyed it. That decision almost destroyed me. It turned out that that man thought he was a living prophet, but I thought he was a dead loss. By contrast, I loved Pastor Alan, I think because we had the same philosophy of life—life is uncertain, eat desert first (at least if Rachel and Rosemary are not around.) He encouraged me to take up my books again and study.

I would like, if the Lord permits, to write on the Pastoral Epistles. First and Second Timothy were written to a young minister doing an intentional interim ministry in the troubled church in Ephesus. To get back into the swing of things I researched the city, its history and its religious setting.[1]

---

1. This work has been revised and released by Wipf and Stock as *Ephesus, The Nursery*

On Appointing a New Pastor

As I read the Biblical references to Ephesus, of course I came to Revelation 2:2–3, the letter to the church in Ephesus, "**2** 'I know your deeds and your labor and perseverance, and that you cannot tolerate evil people, and you have put those who call themselves apostles to the test, and they are not, and you found them *to be* false; **3** and you have perseverance and have endured on account of My name, and have not become weary."

I thought this sounds awfully familiar. These words were probably written as late as the AD 90s, yet thirty years before, these were exactly the charge given by Paul to young Timothy.

Exhortation in Revelation	As Reflected in 1 Timothy
Hard work	Clothed with good deeds 2:10 Train yourself to be godly 4:7 Work hard in your ministry 4:13–16 Fulfilling family responsibilities 5:3–5 The good work of the widows on the list 5:9–10 The young women not to be idle 5:11–14 Church given to charity 5:16 Slaves are to honor their masters, so the faith is not slandered 6:1 The rich are to be rich in good deeds 6:18
Perseverance	Those who wander away (in the negative) 6:10 Continuing in faith love and holiness 2:15 The widow who is alone 5:5 Take hold of eternal life 6:12–14 Taking hold of eternal life through good works 6:19
Discernment	Devoting themselves to myths 1:4 Choosing your leaders Knowing how to conduct yourself in god's household 3:15 The way to treat other Christians 5:1–2 Recognizing those elders worthy of double honor 5:17 Do nothing out of favoritism 5:21 Hidden good deeds show themselves in the character of the giver 5:25 False teachers have the wrong motivations 6:3–5 Godliness and contentment better than wealth 6:6–9 Trust in God not wealth 6:17 Turn away from godless chatter 6:20

of Christianity.

Exhortation in Revelation	As Reflected in 1 Timothy
Endurance	Fight the good fight 1:18 Fight the good fight 6:11 Guard what has been entrusted to you 6:20
Hating the work of evil men	False teachers coming 4:1–2 Those who sin to be rebuked publicly 5:20 Don't share in the sins of others 5:22

Table 2 Similarities between Paul's charge to Timothy and the letter to the Church in Ephesus in Revelation

Can a man's ministry be in evidence many years after his departure? Timothy came to Ephesus to sort out the problems in about 63 AD. Tradition says he ministered and finally died there another 15 years later taking us to about 80 AD. The date of the writing of revelation is disputed, it was probably towards the end of emperor Domitian's reign which was from 81–96 AD. So, we are probably talking about something like thirty years since Timothy's ministry started and fifteen years after it was completed. His ministry cast a long shadow.

I have known those whose ministry departed with them. A good friend was working for me part time while he finished his ministry training. Unfortunately, he injured himself one day, so I took him off to our Christian doctor. He said to my friend that I have a workplace rehabilitation scheme in place, and he would have to be assessed. My trainee minister friend replied, "Don't worry, I am only working two days a week." To which I replied, "That's right John, he is trying to get used to working only one day a week." Sadly, too often the truth is spoken in jest!

Can a ministry last a long time? I have known many ministers over my fifty-six years and of course they all had an influence—not all good—but for me there is one minister whose ministry shaped who and what I am and that was thirty-seven years ago. What of you, can you name one name above all others? I have been described as one of God's concrete Christians, all mixed up and set in my ways. Mixed up? Perhaps, set in my ways? Yes. I do not imagine that the ministry of any new pastor is going to change me into something hugely different to what I am now (mores' the pity Rachel says) and the same goes for all we older members. There are still plenty of edges to knock off to be sure and the continual need for a shepherd is still needed. Thank God we had godly ministers to mold us when we were young.

Our vote today is not to appoint a minister just for the sake of having a minister. Rather we have to ask, "Do we believe that Iain Russell is going to have a ministry that will outlast him?" Do we believe that this man and his wife will correctly mold our youth and new Christians in a way that will be evident fifteen even thirty years from now? If the answer is. "Yes," then he is a man worthy of double honor, honor for the position he carries, and more importantly, honor for a job well done.

This is what we can and must expect of our pastor, but our pastor can expect something from us. I was talking to a friend on Saturday about his church. They are amending that church's constitution to make provision for the removal of the minister. There is no corresponding clause in our constitution for the member who only works at his Christianity one day a week. We have the luxury of having an easy ride if we so wish, just turn up on Sunday and warm a pew and you will get your cup of tea. Surely our minister can expect more of us than that? And our text speaks to us again.

"Realize how far you have fallen. Repent, and do the works you did at first. Otherwise, I will come to you and remove your lampstand from its place, unless you repent."

How far have we fallen as a church? This used to be the place to be, but something went wrong, and we allowed it to go wrong. We have had a service of repentance and that is good and was good. But repentance is more than a single church service. John the Baptist hit the nail on the head when he said Luke 3:8, "Produce fruit in keeping with repentance." This text tells us just what that fruit is, "Do the works you did at first."

I have heard Pastor Alan say a number of times that most of the people who made this church great are still here but there is only one problem; we are all a lot older, perhaps somewhat disillusioned. Disillusioned with people of course, but really any disillusionment is with our Maker himself. Look at our text, "^{2} I know your deeds and your labor and perseverance, and that you cannot tolerate evil people, and you have put those who call themselves apostles to the test, and they are not, and you found them *to be* false; ^{3} and you have perseverance and have endured on account of My name, and have not become weary." Here is a something strange, do the works you did at first, yet you are still doing the works you did at first, you still have endurance, you are still suffering, you are still working hard for Christ. It was not the actions that had changed but rather the spirit it was done in. "Yet I hold this against you: you have lost the love you had at first." The Ephesian church was shell shocked.

The church had changed, going from the early enthusiasm of a fellowship of believers to becoming highly structured. The church had also gone from a period of error held in good faith through to teachers who deliberately lead the members into error. People had fallen away from the faith while others are still resolute in the faith but eventually losing their first love. Tradition tells us that their beloved pastor, Timothy, tried to halt a pagan procession of idols, ceremonies, and songs. In response to his preaching of the gospel, the angry pagans beat him, dragged him through the streets and stoned him to death. Greater heresy would later come from a man called Cerinthus during the ministry of the Apostle John. Polycarp, a disciple of John, remembered what happened when the Apostle came across Cerinthus. John believed Cerinthus's message was so hostile to Christianity that when (and I quote), "John, the disciple of the Lord, (was) going to bathe at Ephesus, and perceiving Cerinthus within, rushed out of the bath-house without bathing, exclaiming, "Let us fly, lest even the bath-house fall down, because Cerinthus, the enemy of the truth, is within."[2] Many people went out from the church because of him. They had just seen the city build a temple to a currently reigning Caesar and then worship a living man, the first such temple in the Roman Empire. The lies that people were believing instead of the precious truth were getting bigger by the year. Shell shocked was probably the best word to describe them.

We have not had to endure anywhere near as much, but I believe we are all in need of renewal and no minister can take us there if we do not wish to go. Daniel Rolands was one of the great leaders of the Welsh revival. It is said of him one night he went to bed an ordinary country clergyman, when he woke up it was as if there was a lion loose in him. Perhaps it might happen here. What history has shown is more likely to happen is, that just a few will meet regularly for prayer for revival. And that a few faithful men and women, themselves not revived can lead a whole church and a whole community back into the vitality of the first love.

Conclusion

The Lord threatened that he would remove the church from his presence, and he did just that, but over six hundred years later. Not before the temple

2. Irenaeus, *Adv. Heresies*. 3.3.4

On Appointing a New Pastor

of Artemis was in ruins, the emperor had bowed his knee, the heresies that threatened the church had passed and the area was thoroughly Christian. Will this church see another 125 years? Who can give account for four generations on, ministers or members? But we can answer a more immediate question, "Is the ministry of this church finished now in 2007 or does the Lord has more work for us to do?" The answer to that is a resounding "Yes."

6

On the Separation of Church and State

Background

THIS SERMON WAS PROMPTED by turmoil in the Australian political system. Christian Prime Ministers had been replaced by an atheist who promoted practices abhorrent to most Christians. At about that time I went to Brisbane with our pastor to a one-day seminar on preaching. One of the speakers, Malcolm Gill, had just completed his doctorate on the interaction of politics and religion in Ephesus. I thought, "Dear Lord, I am not alone in the world after all; there are now two people who find the subject interesting." Much of what I am saying today was prompted by his book *Jesus as Mediator*, a look at the text in its historical setting.

Reading

Isa. 45 1–7, God called Cyrus as his servant.

Text: 1 Tim. 2:1–7.

First of all, then, I urge that entreaties and prayers, petitions and thanksgivings, be made on behalf of all men, ² *for kings and all who are in authority, so that we may lead a tranquil and quiet life in all godliness and dignity.* ³ *This is*

On the Separation of Church and State

good and acceptable in the sight of God our Savior, **4** *who desires all men to be saved and to come to the knowledge of the truth.* **5** *For there is one God, and one mediator also between God and men, the man Christ Jesus,* **6** *who gave Himself as a ransom for all, the testimony given at the proper time.* **7** *For this I was appointed a preacher and an apostle (I am telling the truth, I am not lying) as a teacher of the Gentiles in faith and truth.*

Well, we live in interesting times, don't we?[1] Apparently and old Chinese curse says, "May you live in interesting times." It is possible that we are going to see the greatest attempt of anti-Christian social engineering that our nation has ever seen. How should we as Baptists approach this?

Firstly, have you ever wondered what it means to be a Baptist as opposed to being say, a Presbyterian, a Lutheran, or an Anglican? There is a difference, what does it mean? It means that we are blessed you might say, I won't argue, but what are those distinctives that characterize us? You can get some different answers, what do you think? There isn't total agreement, but it has been defined this way

- Biblical authority (Matt 24:35; 1 Pet 1:23; 2 Tim3:16–17),
- Autonomy of the local church (Matt 18:15–17; 1 Cor 6:1–3),
- Priesthood of all believers (1 Pet 2:5–9; 1 Tim 5),
- Two ordinances (believer's baptism and the Lord's supper) (Acts 2:41–47; 1 Cor 11:23–32),
- Individual soul liberty (Rom 14:5–12),
- Saved church membership (Matt 16:18; Eph 5:23–32; Col 1:18),
- Two offices of the church (pastor and deacon) (1 Tim 3:1–13; Tit 1–2), and
- Separation of church and state (Matt 22:15–22).

Well, they talk about five-point Calvinists, are you an eight-point Baptist, or a seven, or a six or a five? Any less than four you probably come

---

1. Our prime Minister at the time, Julia Gillard was an atheist who moved into "The Lodge," the home of Australian Prime Ministers, along with the "First Bloke." She gained power by an act of gross disloyalty to the then leader. The other de facto "leader" was Senator Bob Brown, leader of the Greens. The Greens held the balance of power and actively sought to promote every ungodly policy you could imagine. As believers we probably could not imagine them!

here because Tenthill Baptist Church has the best morning tea in the valley. Some people would add to this list, and some would take away, but what is this "separation of church and state?" It means the state is not to dictate doctrine, worship style, organization, membership, or personnel for leadership to the church. The church is not to seek the power or the financial support of the state for spiritual ends.

Well, they don't burn Baptists anymore, at least not in Australia. Neither is there a state church so I don't suppose that this is something that we would think about much. But sometimes it is worth remembering that governments have not been the natural ally of our Lord's church. If you have some time, I would urge you to read the early history of the Baptists, I can lend you some books, each page has the waft of smoke and the stain of blood on it along with the rantings of a government or a church in league with a government that said, "We want control of your conscience." "This is how you will think, this is how you will act, and this is what you will accept as truth." Cardinal Hosius, the president of the Council of Trent, (Rome's response to the Reformation) said, ". . . were it not that the Baptists have been grievously tormented and cut off with the knife during the past 1200 years, they would swarm in greater numbers today than all the reformers." All this was done in collusion with the state.

But we are digressing, we have a text, 1 Timothy 2:1–7, and we must return to it. You know, I am glad that when I am speaking from the Pastoral Epistles, I am speaking among friends not theologians. It is said that eighty to ninety percent of theologians believe this book is a fraud. When the scholars who translated the New English Bible came to verse two of 1 Timothy 1, where it says, "Timothy, my true son", they deliberately said "Timothy, his true son" just to put you and me in our place.

Accepted	Frauds
Romans	Ephesians
First Corinthians	Second Thessalonians
Second Corinthians	First Timothy
Galatians	Second Timothy
Philippians	Titus
First Thessalonians	Colossians
Philemon	

Table 3 Authorship of Pauline epistles according to liberal scholars

On the Separation of Church and State

They wanted to remind simple believers like us that they know that our Bible, the Word of God that we put our trust in as a true guide, (remembers the B of Baptist) contains whole books that are just lies, how silly we are. Why do they say this with great authority ("this is the assured results of scholarship." one writer said), particularly when it comes to 1 and 2 Timothy and Titus? Well, they say, among other things, the language isn't Paul's.

Word	Times used in accepted letters	Times used in Pastoral Epistles
Savior	2	10
Appearance	0	6 (Noun and Verb)
Piety	0	13

Table 4 The language of the Pastoral Epistles is wrong apparently

Just look at this table. Yes, the language is different, but they don't ask, what situation would have prompted Paul to write not just with a different emphasis, but with a very different emphasis than in other books. Why? Because it is the language of politics, first century politics maybe, but politics none the less. More to the point it is the language of resistance and sedition!

Place	Reaction
Cypress	Proconsul impressed by Apostles and their message
Philippi	Magistrates apologize to Paul and Silas for beating them
Corinth	Proconsul Gallio pronounces them innocent of any offence against Roman law
Ephesus	Leading officials are friends of Paul's and is absolved of charge of sacrilege
Palestine	Procurators Felix and Festus find Paul innocent of crime. King Herod finds him innocent and not deserving imprisonment.
Rome	Is allowed to carry on his missionary role while under guard.

Table 5 Paul's relations with Rome in Acts

Think for a few moments of how the government, Rome, is portrayed in the gospels. You have the centurion with the greatest faith Jesus had seen and then another centurion acknowledges him as the Son of God at the crucifixion. Pilate fights a hopeless battle against the Jewish leaders to save Jesus. Jesus tells him that his sin is less than those who handed him over. In Acts, Rome is no enemy of the gospel, you have another godly centurion, look at Rome during Paul's travels and how proud he is of his citizenship (you dare to flog a Roman citizen?) and he is prepared to use his citizenship to promote the gospel. The rule of law is upheld and only once is there an unresolved problem. That was when he is in prison in Caesarea. In that case there was only a problem because the governor was corrupt, his successor is scrupulous. Throughout Acts, Rome allows the gospel to progress at best unhindered by the government and is even sometimes very supportive.

56	Paul writes Romans 13:1–7 "Be subject to the governing authorities
63	Paul writes 1 and 2 Timothy and Titus. There are limits to our subjection
64	First persecution under Nero.
81 (or later)	John writes of Rome drunk with the blood of the martyrs

Table 6 Possible Timeline

But, by the time you get to John writing Revelation, when he was a prisoner on Patmos, the picture has changed totally. Here, Rome is now the harlot drunk with the blood of the saints (Rev 17:6).

John's book is a form of writing called "apocalyptic" which means "lifting the veil" or "revelation" but, despite that, it is as if John was lowering a veil over the history of the world. He is not writing something that is easy to read and understand. It is about visions and dreams. Nothing is clear. You imagine when his guards report to their superiors, "What's John up to?" "Don't worry, the old man has lost his mind, he is writing unintelligible nonsense." But when the saints read this same material they say, "Thank you Jesus," because they are in the know. A major consideration in the writing of apocalyptic is safety. We are used to free speech; just think how real the danger was.

On the Separation of Church and State

Tacitus wrote about the first persecution of Christians in his annals about the events surrounding the fire of Rome in AD 64, as little as three years after our text in 1 Timothy:

> Accordingly, an arrest was first made of all who confessed; then, upon their information, an immense multitude was convicted, not so much of the crime of arson, as of hatred of the human race. Mockery of every sort was added to their deaths, covered with the skins of beasts, they were torn by dogs and perished, or were nailed to crosses, or were doomed to the flames. These served to illuminate the night when daylight failed. Nero had thrown open his gardens for the spectacle, and was exhibiting a show in the circus, while he mingled with the people in the dress of a charioteer. Hence even for criminals who deserved extreme and exemplary punishment, there arose a feeling of compassion; for it was not, as it seemed for the public good, but to glut one man's cruelty that they were being destroyed.[2]

That was a long time ago maybe, but Germany seventy years ago wasn't.[3]

Return to our text, *first of all*, now it could mean that the first thing that comes to Paul's mind is pray for the government, but I am certain that Paul is saying, "The most important thing you can do is to pray for those in authority, from the top to the bottom." From Julia down to our local councilors. The emperor would have been happy; "You wander off to your pretty little temples and pray for me. But you make sure you come down to my temple and pray to me." Believe and do whatever you want so long as it doesn't interfere with our agendas and our power.

When Barry and Leone[4] were walking the streets of Ephesus they might have seen an inscription that said "Julius Caesar, the savior of the world." In fact, we know of fifty inscriptions or statues in Ephesus from Paul's time saying something similar, the name of the emperor might change yet three words that keep occurring on them were *savior*, *appearance*, and *piety*. In their coinage the words *savior*, and *appearance* keep re-occurring. Your emperor was the appearance of god on earth. Piety was seen by the Greeks and Romans as a desirable virtue which many tried to achieve but

---

2. Tacitus, *Annals*, 15.44.5–8
3. Or Ukraine in 2022!
4. Members of our church. Leone is the one who makes the lighter than air sponges that make our morning teas so memorable.

it was virtually unachievable, the best you could hope for was the outward acts of participation in the worship of these gods.

If you tell a lie long enough people start to believe it. This is why the Pastoral Epistles are so different. The political environment had transformed in a few short years from what Paul first knew when Artemis reigned supreme. Our political environment is changing too. When Paul writes our text, nothing is hidden in dreams and visions; it is all out in the open. Government, you have overstepped the mark, you are claiming for yourself the power and the glory that belongs to God himself. What is written in 1 Timothy could have got Paul in deep trouble with the authorities. Paul was saying to the Christians living in this changing environment, "Forget everything that you see and hear coming to you from all sides, Jesus is your Savior, Jesus is the appearance of God on earth, Jesus is the mediator of God's blessing of salvation to mankind." We have that word in our text, he is the "Eternal King," (1 Tim 6:14–15). For a Christian, *peace*, again that word is in our text, *peace* does not come from the sword of the legionaries, the *Pax Romana*, but through the church's prayers for those who lead.

For years we have been told lies, different lies for a different century of course, but lies none the less by those in government or who would like to govern. Lies like, "There is nothing wrong with abortion, that men should be allowed to marry men and adopt babies, that all religions and the cultures that get their values from their religions are equal, that we cannot say things from this pulpit that are in accord with God's word but might give offence, that sin does not exist, it's a sickness, or genetics." These lies were appalling and beyond belief when we first heard them, but they have been repeated so often they have become accepted by many and are even mainstream now. Where will it end? How far are we from a time when two men will come to a Baptist minister and say, "Marry us in your church and if you show discrimination against us, we will take your buildings in compensation for our hurt feelings, and you will face the full force of the law that cares nothing for your Christ?" And all we want is a peaceful and quiet life.

So, Paul said to pray for those who rule that you may live these peaceful and quiet lives, but this passage is far more than that. It shouldn't just be a desire for our own wellbeing. We are to pray for everyone in authority because this pleases God. Why? Because through this peace, all men might have the opportunity to know the truth and be saved. Because God gave one mediator as a ransom for all men.

On the Separation of Church and State

Some words of observation if not necessarily practical advice would be in order.

Will a heathen government give us bad government? I am sorry but it doesn't follow. Let me explain. Imagine that when I visit Doctor John[5] and the conversation goes something like this,

"Ted, you have a disease only a dog should catch, I have to send you to a specialist urgently and fortunately there are two available. There is a Dr. Patel."

"Is he any good John?"

"He is a lovely Christian man and full of grace."

"But is he any good?"

"Ted, the man's a butcher."[6]

"Is there anyone else?"

"There is a Dr. House."

"Is he any good?"

"He is an atheist, and he has the bedside manner of a pig."

"But is he any good?"

"There is none better!"

Where would you go? There are some tasks that need ability, and no amount of sanctification is going to compensate. God's help added to ability is far better of course but if you can only have one, which do you choose?

Think of the extremes shown in the Bible about pagan kings. Take Pharaoh, Moses said to him, "Let my people go," but he hardened his heart and God said that he raised him up to proclaim his glory throughout the world. Cyrus, King of Persia said to God's people, "Would you like to go home?" 200 years before he was born God said in Isaiah 45 that he would take him by the right hand and he will anoint him as his servant, his messiah!! It is same word used for Jesus. May there be no doubt, they both did God's will, and both of their hearts were in God's hand. It is just that we would like our governments to do the Father's work willingly.

How should our relations be with individual politicians? Should we remain aloof? You are in league with the Devil, and we do not want to associate with you. Church and state should be separate? Look at Paul in Acts 19, and the account of the riot in Ephesus. The wise heads of his friends who were high officials in the province (19:31) prevented Paul from going

---

5. A church member at the time.

6. Dr. Patel was accused of gross incompetence at the Bundaberg Hospital and served time on three counts of manslaughter.

to the theatre where he could well have been killed. The title Paul's friends had, "Asiarch" was only given to influential men who were at the interface of the Greek city and the government of Rome. Part of their role was to preside over the public games and the religious rites at festivals in honor of the gods and the emperor. They did this at their own expense, so they were wealthy. On two accounts they would be ruled out from "friendship" with Christians, at least as many have come to understand Christianity. Yet Paul called these men "friends", and they treated Paul as a friend. We would be blessed to have the council of such men. May we never be so "holy" that we do not have the unconverted among our friends.

Let me try and draw this to a conclusion. There was a third word, "piety," that virtually unachievable virtue that the pagans struggled to reach without success. It is probably not a word we like to use now. It is too religious, but it is a good word, nonetheless.

Paul tapped into the aspirations surrounding this common word with the meanings of reverence, loyalty towards your parents and your god, and also the fear of god and said, "The high goals you seek are only found in Christ." As Christians, we are to live as model citizens, praying for our government and show what true piety is through our godly living under the true Savior of humanity.

May the Lord grant us that great blessing, a peaceful and quiet life lived in all godliness and holiness.

7

Victorious Christian Living

Text: Revelation 2:1-7

"To THE ANGEL OF the church in Ephesus write:
The One who holds the seven stars in His right hand, the One who walks among the seven golden lampstands, says this:
2 'I know your deeds and your toil and perseverance, and that you cannot tolerate evil men, and you put to the test those who call themselves apostles, and they are not, and you found them to be false; 3 and you have perseverance and have endured for My name's sake, and have not grown weary. 4 But I have this against you, that you have left your first love. 5 Therefore remember from where you have fallen, and repent and do the deeds you did at first; or else I am coming to you and will remove your lampstand out of its place—unless you repent. 6 Yet this you do have, that you hate the deeds of the Nicolaitans, which I also hate. 7 He who has an ear, let him hear what the Spirit says to the churches. To him who overcomes, I will grant to eat of the tree of life which is in the Paradise of God.'

Introduction

Our dear Lord who is patient, loving, kind, understanding and gracious was really ticked off by a group in the Ephesian church called the Nicolaitans.

Sermons from a Potato Field

Now, when I think how patient he is with me that really would take a lot of doing. They get another mention a few verses down when he wrote to the church in Pergamum where we read:

15 So you also have some who in the same way hold the teaching of the Nicolaitans. 16 Therefore repent; or else I am coming to you quickly, and I will make war against them with the sword of My mouth.

I really would not like to have been a Nicolaitan! I wouldn't want anyone here to be one either, but just who were they? They burst onto the scene a long time ago and just as quickly disappeared. Well, I am sad to say, but in this very church, this very day, there is a clue to who they were. Now, there is no point looking to the left of right, I am afraid to say that you will find it behind the pulpit. No, don't look at me either, it's my shoes.

Yes, they are Nikes. I bought them in Jakarta with Vangie,[1] they cost $35 but would have to have paid $50 for top of the line.

Now some of you may own a pair of Doc Martins. (Catherine has even more shoes than Rachel I am told). You would reasonably expect that somebody by the name of Martin, who was a doctor was involved with the founding of the company. It's a reasonable assumption. Likewise, you would expect that someone by the name of Nick was the founder of this company, but not a bit of it. It's ancient Greek.

It means "victor" or "conquer." The old Greeks had a god called Nike, the god of victory. I want you to know these are my victorious shoes. When I wear them, I am invincible. I pity anyone who wears Adidas or Reebok, because, quite simply, they are not "victorious." Consider Michael Jordan; remember how good he was at basketball because he wore Nikes. In fact, I am so convinced of the power of my victorious shoes that if I raced Robert de Castella[2] from the church to the substation[3] and I could wear my victorious shoes and he has on Slazenger's, I would just have to win!

It is at about this stage that one of the wise women of this church, perhaps Heather, either one, should get up, come up here, put her arm around my shoulder and say, "There, there, Ted, have you stopped taking your medication? You have lost your grasp on reality. Beat De Castella to the substation! At your age you are flat out seeing the substation, let alone run there! And as for Michael Jordan, he was good at basketball because he had talent, and dedication, and training and practice, all of which you lack.

1. My daughter
2. Australia's greatest ever marathon runner.
3. A long-standing local landmark.

Victorious Christian Living

Ted, when it comes to being victorious you are talking the talk, but you are not walking the walk."

So that takes us to these Nicolaitans. What do we know about these particularly odious heretics? Apart from the fact that they had some beliefs and some actions that the Almighty despised, we know nothing at all from the scriptures. As for the church fathers, there were some fertile imaginations, and the further they were from the time of the apostles, the more fertile they were. Some said they were disciples of Nicholas of Antioch, one of the deacons of Acts. Now if you listen to Epiphanius of Salamis (c. 320–403 well after the event), Nicholas was a good candidate for a man to lead you astray. You see he did not live a victorious life; he had a beautiful wife and, shame to say, he was quite partial to those special times I am told married couples sometimes share. Every good Christian at that time knew that to live a victorious life you had to live like a monk. When you look around at the children and grandchildren this church has been blessed with, I am grateful our lives in that department is less than victorious. In the end his association with that heresy is somewhat doubtful.

Look at the word. *Nico* means "conquer" in Greek, and *laitan* refers to lay people, or laity; so, the word may be taken to mean "lay conquerors" or "conquerors of the lay people." That is simple enough for me to understand. Suggestions are wild about the implications. Were they the "victorious people?" Or are they victorious over the people, i.e., over the Roman system or even over other Christians as in the establishment of the Episcopal system? Either way it has something to do with living victoriously. And surely, we all want to live victoriously.

There were a couple of the very early church fathers who mention them. Clement of Rome, Pope from c. 92 to c. 99 who was in a position to know and said, ". . . Some are impudent in uncleanness, such as those who are falsely called Nicolaitans." Irenaeus born during the first half of the 2nd century, discusses them, repeats the falsely called Nicolaitans statement but adds nothing to the Apocalypse except that "they lead lives of unrestrained indulgence." So really, we have no idea who they were.

Point 1. Abuses in Attempting to Live a Victorious Life

The point is that they thought that they were victorious, just like me with my shoes, but they had stopped taking their pills. Wiser heads looked on and saw that there was nothing victorious about them at all. In reality, they lived a life of defeat. So, it leads us to the big question, "What is victorious Christian living?" The early church really struggled with this. We have just spoken about poor old Nicholas of Antioch and not many of us met that standard for victorious living. But the church has experimented with different and far more bizarre beliefs in an attempt to live the so called victorious Christian life. And might I say, the church is still experimenting. The expression "victorious Christian living" occurs more than 1 million times if you do a Google search. It is certainly a buzz word (actually, that is three words) spawning umpteen books on the subject. I dare say some of the content of the books on victorious Christian living may be almost as bizarre as past searches for a victorious life. Just how bizarre were they?

The monks and hermits of the fourth and fifth century set new heights as they struggled to live a victorious life. They looked at being victorious through discomfort. Consider these

Conon, a Cilician monk, had a one meal a week for thirty years
Adolus slept only for three hours before dawn, but he was a real slacker
Sisodes spent the night on a jutting crag where sleep meant death
Pachomius only slept standing up

Some ate grass, some lived in rooms too low to stand up, too short to lay down

They looked at being victorious by being filthy. The dirtier they were the holier they were and the more victorious they were.

Simeon Stylites dropped vermin when he walked. Fortunately, he didn't do much of that. He lived for 39 years on a small platform on top of a pillar near Aleppo in Syria. Several other stylites later followed his model. Can you imagine when Iain eventually leaves us, that we decide to take a tack towards being really victorious and we say to our next pastor, "We are renting the manse out so we can send the money to the leprosy mission, and we have put in a post out the back yard for you to live on and practice being victorious?" We would all be locked away.

Jerome who translated the Latin vulgate, wrote to a woman called Paula saying, "Why should Paula add fuel to a sleeping fire by taking a bath? She wrote back, "A clean body and a clean dress mean an unclean soul." Suddenly Christianity became attractive to children.

Anthony never changed his vest or washed his feet

Some tried to be victorious by killing all human relationships and emotions. They really fouled up relationships between men and women:

Victorious Christian Living

Augustine would never see any woman except in the presence of a third party. Mind you it was what I was taught

Pior, an Egyptian monk, was ordered by his superior to see his sister. He obeyed, but he kept his eyes shut tight all the time he was in his sister's presence.

A dying nun refused to see her brother.

Melania, a prominent Roman woman lost her husband and two of her three sons in one week. Her reaction was to thank God, "More easily can I serve thee, O Lord, in that thou hast relieved me of so great a burden."

I found most of these people easily on the internet. They were considered as people who were really special and victorious not only at the time, but some still have their feast day. They were not seen as people who should have been on medication.

Point 2. What is Victorious Christian Living?

You will probably say to me, "Ted its obscene, but it was an awful long time ago. What has it got to do with me now?" It is easy to see what people like that would have thought of the word "pleasure," but that tradition has never wholly died. All that changes is the name, there is always some new form of complete rot or a distorted truth to take its place. In my sixty years I have witnessed legalism, the killing of pleasure, the God is dead movement, the Jesus movement, extreme Pentecostalism, extreme anti Pentecostalism, shepherding movement, positive confession, Toronto blessing, worship movement and there is probably a few more to be added. If the Lord grants me more years, I will see even stranger things. Like these first and third and fourth century aberrations these ideas have come, and most have largely gone, and some new thing is just around the corner. It, and only it will have the secret that has been missing from our lives to allow us to live a victorious Christian life.

Well, we have briefly looked at some victorious Christians that are hard acts to follow, how victorious are you? I don't think they were victorious at all, they were like the Nicolaitans with deeds and doctrines that shouted to the world how victorious they thought they were, but their confidence again, like that of the Nicolaitans, was false. I expect most of you take your membership of this church somewhat for granted as many of you have known no other life. Do you realize what a blessing it is to live here and now and to be free to live a true victorious life free of this rubbish. But you may say, and probably should say, "What is a victorious Christian life?" Well as Baptists we look to the scripture and to the lives of the saints lived in there. My friend David Steer's father was a minister of the Gospel Standard Baptist church. Our victorious Christian lives should be better than gold standard, they should be "gospel standard."

Look at the apostle Peter; here we have a gospel standard to mold a victorious Christian life on. Look at him, he is in a storm, and he gets out of the boat and walks on water! When he starts to sink Jesus comes along and just plucks him out. He has a bad night fishing, and all his hard work doesn't result in a harvest. Then Jesus comes along and just fills up the net. He might not have much money, but he can say rise up and walk! He is put in prison and God just lets him out. Now, wouldn't you say, "That is victorious Christian living." Does your life reach to that standard? Mine doesn't, and yours probably doesn't either. I do not read too many biographies partly because, if their life is significant enough to get into a book, it is probably lived along the model lived by Peter and my own ordinary life is shown for what it is—ordinary. "So, Ted, what do I have to do to live a victorious Christian life, how do I walk on water or are you even in a position to tell me."

Well, I expect most of you already are living one. You see, Peter isn't the only model for victorious Christian living. In our reading the apostle Paul shows a very different life altogether, yet it is still gospel standard just the same. When I was setting the reading, the problem was where to start and end, we could have read all of chapters 11 and 12. Paul is locked up in a city and he escapes down the wall in a basket; the doors don't open for him, and he doesn't just walk past the guards. He gets on a boat and the rats get off (metaphorically speaking), Four times he would be shipwrecked. He spent a night and a day in the water, Jesus didn't come along and pluck him out. He can't even heal himself! There is no miraculous draft of fish, but he must earn his living by the sweat of his brow with all the heartache that goes with that. And on top of that he can't even preach a good sermon, (there is hope for me.) A real apostle would make us pay dearly to listen to their eloquence. And yet, he did escape from Damascus, and yet someone did pluck him out of the sea. He found good friends with a like mind to share the burden of earning a living with. And the sweat of his brow was holy. Yet what we read in 2 Corinthians 11 and 12 sounds awfully ordinary to me and it looked awfully ordinary to others. Paul, how can you call yourself an apostle and expect us to follow you. We don't mind the ATM at the church because we have super apostles to teach us about free grace, why I expect they could walk on water if they had to. In this expectation by others of a life lived in the extraordinary, God came to Paul and said, "My grace is sufficient for you for My power is made perfect in weakness."

The only victorious life there is, is the life that God lives in us, a life where God's strength is made perfect in weakness. So, Ted, are you telling me that my victorious Christian life is no different to that of my non-Christian neighbor? In many ways, "Yes." We experience the same trials, the same joys, the same droughts the same floods, and the same limits that our humanity brings.

Event	Peter	Paul
Both leaders	to the Jews	To the gentiles.
Separate area of work	Jerusalem	Gentile world.
Discourse recorded in full	2:14-40 Pentecost	13:16-42 Antioch of Pisidia.
Healed a lame man	3:1-10	14:8-10
Bought swift judgment	5:1-11 Ananias and Sapphira	13:6-11 Elymas
Freed from prison	5:19-21; 12:1-11	16:19-30
Stressed work of Holy Spirit	2:38	19:2-6
Resurrection primary part of preaching	2:24-36, 3:15, 26, 4:2	3:30-37, 17:3,18,31, 24:15
Both converted a Roman Official	Acts 10	16:25-34
Both appeared before the Sanhedrin	4:1-4, 5:17-21	22:30—23:10

Table 7 Peter and Paul contrasted in Acts

Yet it is very different. Paul could have told a different story in 2 Corinthians, look at this table, Luke, the writer of the book of Acts deliberately makes Paul out to be the equal of Peter. There were times in the ordinariness of Paul's life where God did the extraordinary. Hasn't this been your experience? Hasn't there been times when our Father has drawn so near with a gift of grace that has left you in no doubt that your Heavenly Father loves you and he approves of your life, even if you can't walk on water. I do not know your story but let me tell you a bit of our family's history.

1941 my mother was in hospital in Brisbane dying with blood poisoning. At that time, the US troop convoy arrived in the Brisbane River. Dr. Dolman[4], my father's godfather went and asked the American doctors "Do you have anything new." "Yes! Antibiotics." No mum, no me, no Vangie or Andrew.

In 1950 an Air Force Wirraway aircraft crashed where mum had been sitting minutes before killing relatives she was sitting with. I was only days old and was hungry and wanted to be fed so she took me home. Ross[5] was on the very same beach that same day and witnessed the crash.

During World War Two, a troopship sunk taking all my father in law's fellow trainees, Bob had been detained in England with blanket sores.

My father's mother escaped the Gatton Murders.[6]

What about your story? There will be tales of God's providence that are better than mine. There are times when we realize the extraordinary broke into the ordinary and it was all God's doing and it was all grace.

Conclusion

What do you see when you look back on your life? A life that was lived imperfectly, mine certainly has been. But do you also see God's grace so rich and free poured out upon you? Whose company have you kept? Did you live it talking to and walking with the creator and ruler of this universe? Have you tried to be about his work and his will, I know you have? There is no mystery to living a victorious Christian life. You don't have to live up a pillar for thirty-nine years, you don't have to run after every new fad that comes along, you don't even have to walk on water. We just have to live an ordinary life, but a life lived in God's grace and strength, a life lived in trust

---

4. A much-loved doctor in Gatton a long time ago. He told my father that the most important thing that a doctor in the Lockyer Valley could have was a good horse that could swim. Today you can't even get a house call.

5. One of our number.

6. One of Australia's greatest unsolved crimes. You can find a good article on Wikipedia.

despite the uncertainties of life. And that will turn the ordinary life into the extraordinary. It will be extraordinary simply because it had the approval of the Lord of this universe.

How do we live such a life? Perhaps Mr. Nike got it right after all, "Just do it."

8

Sinners in the Hands of a Gracious God

Background

THIS SERMON WAS PREACHED as the "support act" to a Gideon address. Our pastor was on holiday. How long is it since you had the Gideons in to speak at your church?

Text: Isaiah 32:17

And the work of righteousness will be peace, And the service of righteousness, quietness and confidence forever.

Who is the most spiritual person you know? If we went around this congregation and everybody spoke out the name that is precious to them, I think there would some surprises. Some of you, on hearing a name might say, "I do not know whatever you saw in him or her." What I suspect is that what attracted us to that person above many other worthy brothers or sisters was that their lives showed something that we knew our own lives lacked, something that we wanted. That would be why I expect there would be a different name on each person's lips.

You know, when I was a young man, newly married and just out of Bible college, the person who I would name was, and still do, is Ernie

Sinners in the Hands of a Gracious God

Campbell. What about the Rev. so and so or Pastor such and such? Surely these men of the cloth would have to rate higher than a council truck driver. Let me tell you what I lacked. I had come to Christ in an extraordinary conversion and that could only mean one thing, you become a minister or so I thought. I had wanted to train for the Methodist ministry before trusting Christ (it didn't appear to be a prerequisite there) and now surely this should be the more so now I did trust him. I should continue my plans to study. My foolish thinking was that because God loves the shepherds, he gave them sheep. After years of study, I knew deep inside I was unsuited to be a pastor and my preaching was a persecution of the saints. As I looked at Ernie, I dared to think something radical, that because the Lord loved the sheep, he gave them shepherds. I began to think that the Christian life must be lived in the pews and pity the poor man that has been called to stand this side of the pulpit for the burden is too great except for a man who has been called.

One day Ernie shared his testimony with me. He told me how one day he was out in his truck, and he stopped for lunch at Postmans Ridge[1] near the substation. As he sat there, he looked up in a tree and saw a sign that said, *Jesus Saves*, and as he read it. he knew Jesus was his and he was Jesus's, and his sins were washed away. Of course, there is always more than this, there was a God-fearing wife and going forward at a Billy Graham crusade but in the end, it was just two words, *Jesus saves*. My dear friends, Jesus still saves.

A while back I knew Ernie's time on this world could not be long and I felt a prompting in my spirit, "What are you going to do to honor Ernie and Dulcie who were so good to you when you were young?" I thought, I will purchase a brass instrument for the Gatton Salvation Army band. When the time came, I approached the officer but no, they suggested a drum. Ernie, they said, played the drum and that is important but, more importantly, in the Army, the drum functions as a mobile alter, a place where sinners knelt under the call of the gospel. That is what Ernie would have loved. A heart changed in an inkling.

Pastor Allan and I have referred in the past to Reverend Jonathan Edwards, the congregational minister at the heart of the great awakening in New England in the 1740's. Undoubtedly, he was a great man of God. But if he could bridge the years and look on Ernie's conversion he would say, "I don't think so." Edwards would of course say that it was theoretically possible for God to change a heart in a moment but that is all it was,

1. An area on the road between Gatton and Toowoomba.

theoretical. There is a process that a person must pass through; there are certain boxes to tick before he would give his nod of approval to a man's conversion. Why, if such conversions as Ernie's became common it would be the death of Christianity!

He and likeminded men believed you didn't preach the gospel with a view to converting the listener because that would be letting emotion in the way of a work that was solely the doing of the Holy Spirit. They believed, and I quote, "It was God's usual way and manner, in bestowing grace, to work in the sinners prior to their regeneration in order to reveal their false security and to bring them to a conscious emptiness and need. He must be cast down, confounded, condemned, and cast away, and lost in himself before he will look about for a savior." They were to preach to their consciences with sermons like "The Justice of God in the Damnation of Sinners," or that very famous sermon of his, *Sinners in the Hands of an Angry God*. That way their conscience stares them in the face, so they see the need of a priest and savior and then to know the terrors of Hell. Only such a man who has been through all this can then receive the words, "Believe on the Lord Jesus Christ"

As I read Jonathan Edwards biography over the holidays I thought, "This is scary stuff, here I was, a good Congregational boy, and I had a straight down the line Congregational conversion." I ticked every box, Ross[2], what about you? Bob Knopke a Gatton Gideon who arranges these church presentations is well known to many here. He is an elder in the Gatton Lutherans. You would have to search far and wide for a more faithful brother. He would talk of a different expectation of the journey to faith, one not based on Edward's law but on grace. Here is a fair question, is there a Baptist conversion, a process that everybody will look on and nod approvingly? I expect there is even if you say, "No." What a danger there is in conforming to men's expectations, of weighing one man's journey to faith against our own for we can easily see one or the other as being deficient.

Let's go back to the farming communities of New England where Edwards ministered. Even in a new country the land eventually runs out. What do you do with the second and third son who wants their own farm? No problem, send them to the frontier, and for them it was western New York up near Lake Ontario in the Great Lakes. The fathers wanted to buy the land from people they knew and trusted, which would be one of them

---

2. Ross was bought up a Congregationalist with me. His mother was the organist for many years.

Sinners in the Hands of a Gracious God

who had gone beforehand. So, you had a situation where whole family groups moved from the one valley in New England to another valley on the frontier. It is a bit like finding a valley up Bundaberg way filled with Dorrs, Neuendorfs, Garmeisters, Windolfs and Peipers. The family relationships remained intact, and they carved out their farms and built their Presbyterian or Congregational churches and filled them. And like their parents they would not dare think they were Christian, they wanted to be, and like their parent's ministers, their own ministers would not point them to the gracious Jesus who would forgive their sins, ministers scared witless that they might be quenching the work of the Spirit in conversion. And these sons had to wait and hope that the Lord would come in revival and drag them through the horrors of Hell into the kingdom of Christ. God in his mercy did just that, revival after revival after revival rolled through the valleys of western New York. It became known as the *Burned Over District*.

Burned by the Spirit of God

Would to God that this church was full of men and women who wanted to come to Christ. I know our own pastor would not be backwards in pointing them to a gracious loving and forgiving savior.

I have been speaking about what we expect of ourselves and what others expect of us in our discovery of faith and of our service to the Almighty in the long faith journey that follows. I have been speaking of what we believe makes the Good Lord happy. But probably a better starting point would have been what our Heavenly Father expects of us. And what does he expect of us? I firmly believe that our Lord who says his yoke is easy, and his burden light imposes far fewer demands on us than we impose upon ourselves and others.

I remember some years ago visiting an old friend who was near death. He had lost the confidence of his faith and was in fear of the flames of Hell. Dear Lord, it was so sad. I took my old mentor Eric[3] with me, after speaking to my friend about his soul he said to him, "As a minister of the gospel, and on the authority of God's word I declare to you that if you are trusting Jesus your sins are forgiven, and likewise I declare to you that if you are not trusting Jesus your sins are not forgiven." And it really is as simple as that. Afterwards he asked me, "Was he raised a Presbyterian?" "Yes." He then said he had seen it many times, how some of them just cannot accept grace.

3. The Lutheran pastor in Gatton at the time.

But it is not just a Presbyterian thing, it can be just as much a Baptist thing. All of us have trouble accepting grace. We can be much happier with our list of rules and our check boxes. For Edwards, a child had to become an adult and be dragged crying and even screaming into the bosom of Christ.

But God's word hasn't changed, Jesus had said, "Leave the children alone, and do not forbid them to come to Me; for the kingdom of heaven belongs to such as these." All he wants from you, and me is the same simple trust that children give to their parents who love them and everything else is of grace. And in our weaker moment we have to admit that even that trust is of grace. What does he want? Micah 6:8 says it all, "He has told you, mortal one, what is good; And what does the Lord require of you, but to do justice, to love kindness, and to walk humbly with your God?" Ernie taught me I did not have to be a minister to walk humbly with my God. You can do it just as well driving a truck, or planting potatoes, or even selling timber, don't worry Iain, you can also do it as a pastor.

"Ted that sounds like easy believeism to me." Let's be perfectly frank, for most of us, on most days it is easy, it just comes so naturally. As Isaiah says, "And the work of righteousness will be peace, And the service of righteousness, quietness and confidence forever." We have been blessed to know the quietness and to know the trust that comes from God, not man saying you are righteous because your sins are forgiven. But there are also days when it is very hard believeism and it can take every bit of faith we can muster to trust our Lord in the providences of life. There are days when there is no quietness in our spirit and on such days what rule could you possibly keep to make things different, it is still all of grace.

Dear old Calvin said on the subject of conversion that there could not be less grace in the new covenant than there was in the old, he went on to say that just as Jewish parents have Jewish children, so Christian parents have Christian children. But he was right about there not being less grace in the new than the old and the old says, "Choose you this day whom you will serve," and we are still called to choose. Have the words *Jesus saves*, burned into your heart? Some of you will look at me and say, "Ted, you are forty years too late for that message of choosing." But it is never too late to hear that the Jesus who saved your soul forty years ago can still be trusted with your soul today, and you can trust him with it tomorrow. Sometimes we still have to choose who we will trust and choose who we will serve.

I had a dreadful week at work last week. It is probably not going to be much better this week. Pray for me. I look out my office window and I see

Sinners in the Hands of a Gracious God

a sign, "Massage, and coffee," and I think, Lord that is just what I need. But it is a massage with extra services, "Can we read your cards, do you want to consult a medium?" If you wanted tea instead of coffee, they probably use loose tea and not tea bags so they can read them too. "We have crystals that are really good for losing weight." And I choose, rather to carry the stress of today and trust my Lord with my soul and trust him with whatever tomorrow holds. What of you?

9

The Temple of Artemis

Background

THE SERMON WAS PROMPTED by the completion of the last essay for the set work for my Master of Theology in Applied Theology. The subject of the essay was *The Role of the Holy Spirit in the Pastoral Epistles*. A few days before there had been an unspeakable tragedy on a farm near the church. Reg and Heather visited the family.

First Text: 1 Timothy 3:14–16.

[14] *I am writing these things to you, hoping to come to you before long;* [15] *but in case I am delayed, I write so that you will know how one ought to conduct himself in the household of God, which is the church of the living God, the pillar and support of the truth.* [16] *By common confession, great is the mystery of godliness:*

> *He who was revealed in the flesh,*
> *Was vindicated in the Spirit,*
> *Seen by angels,*
> *Proclaimed among the nations,*
> *Believed on in the world,*
> *Taken up in glory.*

The Temple of Artemis

Second Text: 2 Timothy 1:12–14

12 *For this reason I also suffer these things, but I am not ashamed; for I know whom I have believed and I am convinced that He is able to guard what I have entrusted to Him until that day.* **13** *Retain the standard of sound words which you have heard from me, in the faith and love which are in Christ Jesus.* **14** *Guard, through the Holy Spirit who dwells in us, the treasure which has been entrusted to you.*

On Christmas day I sent off to the UK the last essay for the set work for my course. It was entitled *The Role of the Holy Spirit in the Pastoral Epistles*. As my head had been down and tail up for months, it seems reasonable that this morning's sermon should be drawn from this study.

Our passages are from two letters written by Paul to his apprentice, Timothy who had been sent to Ephesus to sort out a troubled church. This is the earliest Intentional Interim Ministry. This morning we are going to try to enter the world of Paul and Timothy and his young Ephesian church.

Me somewhere exotic in 1970

Back in 1970, I was a slim and fit apprentice motor mechanic. Young men let that be a warning to you, you too can have a body like mine. I had not travelled much further than Lismore to the south and Mooloolaba to the north. But then I went on the adventure of a lifetime, seeing the world, Hong Kong, Ceylon, India, East Africa, the Channel Islands, France, England, Scotland, and Wales. I had seen anything that could be seen for free and in the United Kingdom which was a lot.

I explored buildings that would just blow your mind away, St. Paul's, Westminster Abbey, The Tower, and various cathedrals. I was bitten badly by the travel bug as you know. Unfortunately, the apprenticeship board heard of my absence and my parents were told that if I wasn't back within six months my indentures would be cancelled so there was a frantic rush home via Greece and Hong Kong again.

Sermons from a Potato Field

Stoa of Attalos, Athens

After a couple of days sightseeing in Greece, I went down to the agora, the old market of ancient Athens. Nothing could have prepared me for what I saw, in the colonnade of a building called the Stoa of Attalos. The Stoa was rebuilt in the 1950's to faithfully recreate the original classical Greek building that stood there. It was breathtaking in its simplicity and its beauty. Nothing I had seen over the previous six months compared. When I built "Elim"[1] I tried to capture some of the symmetry that so profoundly affected me that day. I looked up through the pillars at the ruins of the Acropolis and wondered just what Athens would have been like when Paul addressed the philosophers on Mars Hill, now all just a ruin.

Take yourself back almost 2000 years when Paul walked into Ephesus, the third or fourth largest city in the Roman Empire. Its prosperity was built largely on having one of the great harbors in the Mediterranean. It was a planned Greek city (even though it was in Turkey) at the peak of its prosperity. It was all old hat for Paul but if we could see it, we wouldn't believe what we were looking at because of its beauty, its commercial area was all built with or clad in stone. Ephesus was a society as ordered as its architecture, but for all its order it was not renewed by the gospel of Christ.

---

1. The name of our home.

The Temple of Artemis

Outside of the town walls was the Artemision, the temple of Artemis with hundreds of workers, it was the other major source of the city's prosperity. Antipater of Sidon, (second century BC) who compiled the famous seven wonders of the ancient world said of the temple of Artemis, "I have set eyes on the wall of lofty Babylon on which is a road for chariots, and the statue of Zeus by the Alpheus, and the Hanging Gardens, and the Colossus of the Sun, and the huge labor of the high pyramids, and the vast tomb of Mausolus; but when I saw the house of Artemis that mounted to the clouds, those other marvels lost their brilliancy, and I said, 'Lo, apart from Olympus, the sun never looked on aught (anything) so grand." Did he exaggerate the Artemision's beauty?

Column base from the temple of Artemis

Sermons from a Potato Field

If you have been to the British Museum, you might have seen this pillar base from that temple that just hints at its beauty. Pliny the Elder describes the temple "The entire length of the temple is four hundred and twenty-five feet, and the breadth two hundred and twenty-five. The columns are one hundred and twenty-seven in number, and sixty feet in height, each of them presented by a different king"

Meanwhile, after being thrown out of the synagogue, Paul rented the lecture hall of Tyrannus and, when he was not working as a tent maker to make ends meet, preached Christ. To the inhabitants of Ephesus, Paul's God was just another religion competing for the hearts and minds of the residents of this great city along with Aphrodite, Apollo, Asclepius, Athena, Cabiri, Dionysus, Demeter, Egyptian cults, Ge, God most high, Hecate, Hephaestus, Hercules, Mother Goddess, Pluton, Poseidon, and Zeus. Through Timothy, Paul spoke to that small group of probably mostly poor people, meeting in private homes. He dares to say to that insignificant group "You are God's household," or as it may equally be translated, and I believe indented, "You are God's Temple." Across the years to our ordered but unrenewed society, God's word comes to a little church in a potato field, you are God's temple. It doesn't look it to our ordered but unrenewed society. It didn't look like it then either. Paul, can't you see the evidence of your eyes, "Great is Artemis of the Ephesians," they would cry. Ephesus and its temple looked so solid and all so permanent, but Paul knew his God and he would reply, "Great is the mystery of godliness."

Where Ephesus was sighted in Turkey there were many earthquakes and Turkish builders were probably no better then than they are now. The city was constantly being badly damaged but not the Artemision, they planned ahead. Pliny wrote "A marshy soil was selected for its site, in order that it might not suffer from earthquakes, or the chasms which they produce. On the other hand, again, that the foundations of so vast a pile might not have to rest upon a loose and shifting bed, layers of trodden charcoal were placed beneath, with fleeces covered with wool upon the top of them." It was built in a swamp with charcoal and fleeces for a foundation!! The temple was impressive, but it had no foundation! To the Ephesian church he wrote, you are the "foundation of the truth" you are the pillars of the truth. May the church in the potato field never forget that, despite its small size and the way it appears to our community, it is the pillar and foundation of the truth and has been a herald to it for many generations.

The Temple of Artemis

Our second verse also has allusions to the temple. "**12** But I am not ashamed, for I know the one in whom I have put my trust, and I am sure that he is able to guard until that day what I have entrusted to him. **13** Hold to the standard of sound teaching that you have heard from me, in the faith and love that are in Christ Jesus. **14** Guard the good treasure entrusted to you, with the help of the Holy Spirit living in us."

The temple that Paul saw was not the first large temple on the site. The earlier temple was destroyed; it was claimed, by an arsonist in 356 BC on the very same night that Alexander the Great was born. The excuse given for Artemis not looking after her temple was that she was too preoccupied with Alexander's delivery to save her burning temple. Paul came to Ephesus with a radical notion, his God can multi-task. Can your God multitask or is he like Cicero's in his apology for Jupiter's neglect of the world who said that, "The sovereign of the universe is on the whole a good sovereign, but with so much business on his hands that he has not time to look into details?" I ask this because recently just up the road an unspeakable tragedy occurred. Bless you Reg and Heather for visiting this heartbroken family. Was the God who cares for the good people who meet in the potato field too busy to care for the newcomers to our valley? Preoccupied? Too busy? I don't believe it, but I do not understand it, and they never will. Never forget that Christianity was a message of hope in a brutal and bloody age where children died like flies, and it was rare to make old bones.

The image of Artemis in the temple had the signs of the zodiac and a powerful magical spell known as the Ephesian letters carved into it. Her followers believed they didn't need to be affected by astrological fate as she was able to help them and give advice about the future. Through her control of magic and the spirit world they could virtually guarantee to be able to change their fate for good and their enemies for ill.

But Paul preached a God and Savior who through suffering of greatest of tragedies has earned the right to be trusted. A savior, who through the Holy Spirit would be active in their lives protecting them. When this message that God could be trusted with tomorrow finally got through to the Christians of Ephesus, they bought out and burnt spells to the value of 50,000 days wages. Have you learned that God can be trusted with tomorrow?

Our passage also deals with intergenerational transition. I thought about whether I should include this, but I feel it is too important a subject to just skim over. If you ever have me back, I think that we will return to this text.[2]

Paul spoke of the deposit, which was given to him and Timothy and which was to be passed on. It was a very broad term encompassing all their life and ministry. He used a word rich with meaning for the Ephesians. It was used of money placed in their magnificent temple for safe keeping. The temple was also a big bank with over 400 bookkeepers keeping tabs on the loans and deposits. One writer said, "You know the Ephesians, of course, and that large sums of money are in their hands, some of it belonging to private citizens and deposited in the temple of Artemis, not alone money of the Ephesians but also of aliens and of persons from all parts of the world, and in some cases of commonwealths and kings, money which all deposit there in order that it might be safe, since no one has ever yet dared to violate that place. Although countless wars have occurred in the past and the city has often been captured. They [the Ephesians] would sooner, I imagine strip off the adornments of the goddess than touch this money." But their financial prosperity was built on charcoal and fleeces just like the world's economy has proven to be of recent months

What you have put on trust with your maker, and that is guarded with the help of the Holy Spirit is far safer than the money in that temple. It is far safer than a fixed deposit in the National Australia Bank guaranteed by Kevin.[3]

When the archaeologists went searching for the mighty port of Ephesus in the 1800's they found it eight kilometers inland, when the great temple, the glory of the whole world was uncovered it had sunk six metres under the surface of the swamp. So much so for the illusion of permanence. Even though it looks so permanent this whole world will pass away just as Paul's did. Let us never forget that.

Tomorrow I am starting next year with virtually an empty order book. How are your prospects for 2009? I only know this, as for the future we do not need astrology or magic. King George 6th in his Christmas broadcast in 1939, in the darkness of the war said these words.

"I said to the man who stood at the gate of the year

'Give me a light that I may tread safely into the unknown.'

And he replied,

---

2. This is dealt with in the sermon, *The Election of Church Officers*.

3. Kevin Rudd. Our Prime Minister at the time. During the GFC the Australian Government guaranteed bank deposits.

The Temple of Artemis

'Go into the darkness and put your hand into the hand of God that shall be to you better than light and safer than a known way!'"

These words now mark his grave and the grave of Queen Elisabeth the Queen Mother. What will be your epitaph?

All that will remain is that which is built on the foundation of Christ and true wealth is that which is sent ahead. Our Lord has never asked that we see him clearly, just that we trust him.

10

Sermon on the Election of Church Officers

Background

THIS SERMON WAS GIVEN prior to our election of church officers and a proposed constitutional change that would have allowed women deacons. The change was passed. This sermon continues matters flagged in the preceding sermon, *The Temple of Ephesus*.

Reading

2 Timothy 1:8–14. The appearing of our Savior.

Text: 2 Timothy 1:12–14

12 For this reason I also suffer these things, but I am not ashamed; for I know whom I have believed and I am convinced that He is able to guard what I have entrusted to Him until that day. 13 Retain the standard of sound words which you have heard from me, in the faith and love which are in Christ Jesus. 14 Guard, through the Holy Spirit who dwells in us, the treasure which has been entrusted to you.

Sermon on the Election of Church Officers

The last time I had the privilege of preaching here I spoke from two texts, drawing on my studies from the previous year. One of the texts I used was 2 Timothy 1:13–14, and I said at that time that we may return to this text should I be asked to preach again. I spoke of other matters arising from the text that time,

I noticed how it also touches on the very important subject of handing the church on to the next generation. Over following months, the impression became quite strong that I should definitely make this the subject of my next sermon. Soon we will be taking nominations for leadership positions, so it is probably timely. But what makes me a little apprehensive is that next week we are to discuss whether this handing on of the care of the church will involve handing it on to women, and if so, what is the extent of this handover.

Why should I be apprehensive? As some of you know I have just about completed a 20,000-word essay on the role of women's ministry in First and Second Timothy.[1] In this essay I came to a different conclusion to the views held by some of you, views that we both hold in good faith and good conscience as being scriptural and in accordance with the mind and nature of our God. Being the courageous speaker that I am, I decided that the best way to deal with it is to leave it to wiser and more capable people than myself next week. But I will not back totally away from it. If I did, I would not deserve to stand this side of a pulpit ever again.

Paul knows that his present imprisonment will be his last and that he is facing imminent death at the hands of the Romans. So, he said to Timothy, "The time of my departure has come. I have fought the good fight, I have finished the race, I have kept the faith," (2 Tim. 4:6–8). By any standard, Paul had lived a remarkable life, it was said in Ephesus about the Christians that they had turned the world upside down. What they could have said was, Paul, you have turned the world upside down. But elsewhere he calls himself Paul, the aged. If the Romans hadn't taken his life from him, age, and the abuse his body received would surely have caused his body simply to stop. Yet despite the defection of some of those he trusted (1:15), Paul in verse twelve confesses his belief that God can guard what the apostle has entrusted to him, his life, his apostolic ministry, his converts, his churches, his teaching. Paul was passively laying down the baton and entrusting the fruits of his ministry to the last day. This would not be a defeat but his final act of faith,

---

1. Now expanded and revised and published by Wipf and Stock as *Women in Ministry*.

as he says, "... for I know whom I have believed, and I am convinced that He is able to protect what I have entrusted to Him until that day."

My friends, there is a message in our passage to our elders, or anyone who would be an elder. To desire to be an elder is a good thing but it is a ministry that you must be called to, not to just take it upon yourself. This is not a role that someone should enter lightly. Some years ago, when I was fulfilling that role in Gatton Assembly of God, we made a disastrous appointment of a minister. The burden of that responsibility nearly broke me. But our passage is not about taking up the ministry or how to fulfil it but about laying it down.

Equally important as listening to God's voice in accepting the call to eldership is to hear his voice when he says to stand down. As with Paul, even so with lesser mortals such as us, there is a time to pass the baton on to another. Now I have no reason to believe than an entrenched eldership is or has ever been a problem in this church, but I know of some churches where it has been, where an entrenched, and may I add, even at times unspiritual eldership hindered, rather than helped a church. Joy asked me last week if I thought changes in church offices should be gradual. The real danger is it is so gradual it is imperceptible.

Many of you can probably picture a church where this has happened and sadly you probably all have a different church in mind. It can be very easy for elders to consider their church as almost their own possession, something that they have to guard rigidly, as if its future depends only on them. One church that comes to my mind, I expect the attitude was, this was our fathers church and now it is ours and it's our money that is paying the bills. Again, I stress it is not this church that I am thinking of. But we have heard the message often enough of late, my friends, this church, and every church is Christ's church. He is able to guard this church, and he is the only one who can guard what you entrust to him, and we will have to do that one day, one way or the other.

There is one task that an elder never ever stands down from. The really important work that an elder does is not to rule, or better to lead the church, but it is to show us what Christ is like by being Christlike. The guidelines given for eldership in 1 Timothy 3 are not qualifications to be a leader but qualifications to be a role model! Church officers had progressed from imitating the apostles as they in turn imitated Christ to being an example themselves.

Sermon on the Election of Church Officers

13 *"Hold on to the example of sound words which you have heard from me, in the faith and love which are in Christ Jesus."*

When you read the commentaries and books on the Pastoral Epistles, they keep referring to the Ephesian heresy. But for all of that, we really have very little idea of what was going on. Paul does not even bother to attack it. There was no need. The church was no longer in the hands of men who had sat at the feet of Jesus, who had a special calling and anointing and authority to define what sound teaching was. The truth had been defined. In the Pastoral Epistles Paul, on five occasions, quotes five "faithful sayings" and recites a hymn. Our faith is something that is lived but it is never, "No creed but Jesus." It is equally something that is believed. I have not heard a debate about core doctrine since I came, nor do I expect to.

Paul's concern is that truth is not subjective but that there is an identifiable core, beyond which the church cannot stray and still be identified as Christian. At times it is difficult to determine the boundaries of belief. Notwithstanding this difficulty, the core is to be diligently guarded in word and deed by a church and its officers, instructed not only in doctrine but also in how to live a life that demonstrated the "mystery of godliness." This sound teaching can be known equally well by a man or a woman, even a child and all are expected to know it.

14 *"Protect, through the Holy Spirit who dwells in us, the treasure which has been entrusted to you."*

While Paul was laying down the baton and committing the fruits of his ministry to the loving care of God, his charge to Timothy is exactly the opposite. It is now Timothy's responsibility rise to the challenge to actively guard this same treasure now passed on to him in trust. It has now been passed on to us in trust over some sixty to seventy generations. But we do not do it alone because the Spirit is helping. Just as Timothy has access to his supernatural empowerment, so do we. Some take Paul's words about the Spirit living in "us" as referring to their shared ministry gift, a holy select huddle. Rather we should see the universal gift of the Spirit among believers. The Spirit's indwelling of Timothy to guard the gospel is the same indwelling that his mother Eunice, and grandmother Lois had known and for Timothy himself prior to this charge coming upon him (1:5).

It falls to some in the church to be seen to be more actively involved in guarding this treasure, our pastor, elders, and deacons. The qualifications for deacons are only slightly if actually any lower than for elders. The qualifications for elders required that they be proved blameless and faithful in the Christian community. This means that there had to be some level of prior ministry or function before becoming elders. In this way our deacons can be seen as apprentice elders, where evidence of ministry and an exemplary life can be seen. It is a place for the church to see how these men guard the good treasure that has been given to them.

Well, that is the elders and deacons taken care of. Young men, you can just sit back there for another ten or so years and take it easy. All the positions are filled by us oldies. I don't think so! With all the talk about raising the pension age to sixty-seven, it was said that when the pension was introduced that only 10 percent of men ever lived long enough to receive it. Two generations ago these roles would have already fallen upon your shoulders. Paul passed on his ministry to Timothy, but it didn't stop there, he went on (2:2) to urge his apprentice to entrust this same deposit to faithful men. Now you must wait yet you must be those faithful men to whom the church can in turn be entrusted. And this church can have no greater protection than the next generation of men who already have of exemplary lives and who know their faith intimately.

The theologians talk about function and office. Pastor Iain has both function and office. But you do not have to have a title to be about the Lord's business. When Mark and Kylie went to the Scripture Union camp, they didn't phone the elders and ask permission to go, they just did it. This is one of the joys of being a Baptist. I urge you to find that ministry only you and your wife can do; function before you have office. Well, what should I do? It is really not that difficult. I remember one lecturer telling us the need is the call and the Lord will very quickly lay a need upon your hearts if you let him. Be sensitive to it, respond to it.

But what shall we say about our women? I saw a poster once that said, "For a woman to be considered the equal of a man she has to be twice as good." It went on to say, "Fortunately that is not very difficult." Well, I am not going to go down that track, but I will ask, gentlemen, brothers, have you ever seen such a group of capable women in all your life? None of us has married down and I suspect we have all married up. The women of Tenthill Baptist Church are not the silly weak women (2 Timothy 3:6) that were giving Paul and Timothy so much grief. Back then Greek women were given just enough education to cook and have babies and were married off by the time they were fourteen. How could these women be anything other than weak and silly? Coming from a life in paganism they could only know the gospel at best imperfectly. If the woman was Jewish, it wasn't much

Sermon on the Election of Church Officers

better for them either. She could attend the synagogue, but it was better that she be at home. She could listen to the law being read and taught but she was not to learn. To teach a woman the Law was as great a sin as teaching her harlotry. (I actually found the reference.)

No, the women here are great cooks, and they have done a wonderful job of raising their children, but they are not weak and silly. They are strong and capable and more like Priscilla. She could take the preacher Aquila aside and along with her husband teach him the gospel correctly, or any of the nine other women who are commended in the greetings in chapter 16 of Romans. Two of these women had ministered so closely with Paul that they had suffered imprisonment, one is called a minister or deacon and another an apostle.

So, let's conclude and try to draw all these threads together.

We are going to choose church officers very soon and continue the process of handing the care of this church on. Inevitably we are going to give people titles, and they are positions that the Lord takes seriously and for which he gives grace. Paul says of the humble deacon, that those who serve well as deacons gain a good standing for themselves and great boldness in the faith that is in Christ Jesus. So, we thank God for those who have served well, for those who are serving well now. In anticipation we thank him for those who serve well over the coming years.

While it is important to thank God for those who combine office and function our greatest joy and hope for the future of this church should come from those who minister without any office. Reg is no longer officially an elder, but he functioned as an elder during that unspeakable tragedy. That family saw what Christ was like and we as his church family saw what Christ was like. Standing down did not free him from the role to which God had called him. When Mark and Kylie went to the Scripture Union camp, they were demonstrating the faithfulness that must be demonstrated by our future elders and deacons.

As for our ladies, they have been functioning without office for years. But there remains one very good reason for not changing things. In their faithfulness they would end up doing all the work.

11

Repent from Your Wicked Ways

Background

A MUCH LOVED AND very saintly couple and long-standing members of the church were retiring and moving away. The service was followed by a farewell lunch.

Reading

2 Chronicles 7:8–14.

Text: 2 Chronicles 7:14.

"and [if] My people who are called by My name humble themselves, and pray and seek My face, and turn from their wicked ways, then I will hear from heaven, and I will forgive their sin and will heal their land."

Introduction

I have known a number of you for many years but about twelve months ago the relationship changed from friendship to that special bond that exists between members of the same local church. And, as a friend and brother in

Repent from Your Wicked Ways

the Lord the time has come to talk to you about your "wicked ways." What does our text say, "Forsake your wicked ways and turn to God in prayer and it will rain, and you won't have any pests on your crops?"

Point 1. Are We Wicked?

There is only one problem, as I look over each of you gathered here, I do not see too many of you that are wicked. Lady Macbeth was wicked, "Come, you spirits that tend on mortal thoughts, unsex me here and fill me, from the crown to the toe, top-full of direst cruelty!" Many of the Iraqi's, Afghani's and Arabs have proven to be wicked. We are confronted daily with wickedness like we could never have imagined a few short years ago. My son in law is leaving soon to return to Afghanistan–Lord, keep them all safe, but is this a gathering of the wicked of Tenthill? You might be thinking, "Ted, you do not know us too well, if you knew what I know about the person in the pew opposite you wouldn't be quite so generous." Perhaps, but I doubt it. Look at our congregation, Eric and Leah travel from Kentville. There must be twenty churches that are closer, John and Trish travel from Toowoomba, there has got to be fifty closer churches. What of the locals, are you only here because your father, grandfather or even great grandfathers were members? If this really was a synagogue of Satan, you all have enough integrity to shake the dust of this place from off your feet. As for myself?

What are you saying? That we are perfect? Years ago, Greg and I had a run in with a certain man. I remember my old friend Eric[1] telling me how this man had told him he hadn't sinned for two years! What would he say to you? I know it would be, "Forsake your wicked ways!" Imagine, if you will, the marriage feast of the lamb with the standard such people have set for God's acceptance of sinners. There he will be, just Jesus and him, and set before him is a Big Mac, Pizza Hut pizza, and Kentucky Fried Chicken. "Jesus, is this how you reward all my hard work? I was expecting something a bit better than this for such an auspicious occasion." The reply comes back "You don't think I was going to cook for just the two of us, did you?" But it is not going to be like that at all. At that great banquet there will be a countless throng, all of them sinners who know that they are sinners all of them who know the source of forgiveness. I would not be surprised, as I

---

1. The Lutheran pastor in Gatton for many years.

have said previously, if the great chef doesn't come up to Joan and ask her for her recipe for lemon meringue pie for dessert.

But is my judgment of what is and what isn't wicked valid? It is a fair question. God has said your ways are different to mine. Perhaps, if for a moment, I could get a look through the eyes of God I would see something different. But how different are our Heavenly Father's ways from ours? If his ways are different in nature, it means that we, who are supposed to be his children and made in his image, can never know him. And yet our Father wanted us to know him so much that he sent his Son to live among us, to show us his nature, and through Jesus show us how to live. There would not be one of us here that does not have to battle our humanity. Sometimes we win, sometimes we lose, but that does not make us wicked. I want to show you some drawings, what do we have here—is it a square, triangle, octagon?[2]

It is obviously an attempt to draw a circle. It is something that is very hard to do. Each of the children has in mind clearly what they are aiming for, they know the difference between a triangle and circle, not one of these drawings can be confused for anything other than a circle. But they are not round. They differ in degree, not nature. As we grow in grace and maturity, these poor impressions we make of God's dear Son, start having the bumps and dips pushed and pulled. This can all be very painful at times, but after time the circle of a child starts to look more like the circle of a great artist.

It would be easy to tell you that our text says that all we at Tenthill Baptist church have to do to solve our problems here at is to turn from our wicked ways and the creeks will run and the pests will be gone, but it is not the case. As I look out over you, the word that comes to my mind is "faithful," not "wicked." Today is, after all, a celebration of the faithfulness of Wilf and Joan.

It is not to say that there are not wicked people in the district—but as for you!

If our text is not a rebuke to us, what can it say? It says far more than we can ever explore in a month of Sundays. On another day we could look at how as God's people we still need to be humble and how we have been given prayer to bring an unwilling people before Almighty God and ask that the same grace be shown to them as has been shown to us. But today's circumstances lead us in a different direction.

---

2. The children had previously attempted to draw me circles.

Repent from Your Wicked Ways

Point 2. A Time of Transition

This was a message from God to Solomon at the time of transition for the king. The context of the story begins with the dedication of the temple in verse eight and then you have God appearing to Solomon during the night in verse twelve. Just image the great day of the dedication, the fire of God fell and burnt up the offering. The priests could not enter the temple because the glory of the Lord filled it. How would you be that night? High as a kite, in the best sense of the word? Wouldn't that be the best time to hear from God? Perhaps, but that is not when it happened. This happened after the temple and the palace had been built. Second Chronicles 7:11 "Solomon completed the house of the Lord and the royal palace; he successfully accomplished everything he had planned to do in regard to the house of the Lord and his own house."

In 1 Kings 6:37—7:1 we read, "**37** In the fourth year the foundation of the house of the Lord was laid, in the month of Ziv. **38** And in the eleventh year, in the month of Bul, that is, the eighth month, the house was finished in all its parts and in accordance with all its plans. So, he was seven years in building it. **7:1** Now Solomon built his own house over the course of thirteen years, and he finished all of his house."

There is a gap of thirteen years missing between the verses and you can change a lot over thirteen years. He was no longer high; in fact, I think he was quite low. For twenty years Solomon has been working on this project, but before that David his father had started the planning and getting the materials ready. He would have lived and breathed this project from his youth and David drummed into him this is what you must do (1 Chr 29). Solomon has spent all his adult years working on these buildings, they would be two of the most imposing structures in the ancient world, but now it's done, no more to do. The painters have moved out and the landscaping is done. His father's wealth, his own wealth and the wealth of the kingdom had been directed to this task for twenty years. What is left to do? Marry another wife or two, make a few more million, and sign a few more treaties. He had plenty to do; he was, after all, the king but being busy is not the same as working with a purpose and direction. But what has consumed him for his adult life is finished, that chapter has been written and a new one has been opened but it's blank. These were days when men lived very short lives. At about forty he was already an old man, but God had promised him a long life, his life could be more than just the temple and the palace. The thought on his mind was, has my life's work to date counted for anything and what do I do with the remainder of my life. Have you ever thought this also? Perhaps this is the first recorded midlife crisis.

As Solomon prayed that night the Lord assured him that his life's work to date has not been futile. Lord, we all need to hear that the things we have done for love of you were not in vain. Soon this church will be affirming the life of Wilf and Joan. But what of his concern, "What shall I do?" God heard the king that night and came to him, just as he did many years ago at the tabernacle at Gibeon when he was first made king. The reply was not, "This is what you should do," but "This is how you should live."

Wilf and Joan are going through a transition, perhaps you have been asking over recent months what will we do? If the drought continues some of you may well be asking, "What will we do? All that I have known all my working years has all changed." Surely the answer is the same for us as for the great king, "This is how you shall live." I go back to that childlike circle, keep knocking the dints out.

Point 3. Work at What You are Good at

In 2 Chronicles 1:7-12 we read how twenty years previously, the Lord appeared to Solomon and told the young king to ask of him whatever he wanted. The young man asked for the wisdom and knowledge that only age and experience can bring. The Lord told Solomon that he could have asked for wealth, riches and honor and the death of his enemies but because he got his priorities right, he was going to give Solomon wealth, riches, and honor. He had no promise about his enemies being removed.

I cannot come to you with some simple formula like "If you forsake your wicked ways" then the enemy, not just of Tenthill but now much of Australia will be ushered away. And yes, there is much wickedness in our nation, and, Dear Lord, you know our land needs to be healed. What can I say? What the Lord spoke to Solomon that night was not a call to personal repentance, though others may need to, nor was it a call to seek God's face, though others may need to. For while others seek God's face, he had found it and in the finding came a responsibility. The Lord simply said, "As for you, walk before me" and I say to us all, "As for you, continue to walk before him."

But what shall we do? Is there nothing practical from our text? Jack xxxx[3] gave me some advice years ago on how to become a millionaire. It was actually good advice, given to him by a very rich man. He said, "Find

---

3. The mention of this name got everybody's attention.

Repent from Your Wicked Ways

out what you are good at and do lots of it." In the next chapter of Chronicles, after the Lord finished speaking, we see that Solomon realized what he was good at and did lots of it, of course it was building. For most of us our future will be a continuation of doing what we are good at—in all aspects of our life.

12

The Best Use of Life is Love

Background

THIS SERMON WAS ONE of a series which were part of the *Forty Days of Love* program. It was given on Anzac Day; the day Australians remember and honor our fallen.

Text: 1 John 4:7-21

7 *Beloved, let's love one another; for love is from God, and everyone who loves has been born of God and knows God.* 8 *The one who does not love does not know God, because God is love.* 9 *By this the love of God was revealed in us, that God has sent His only Son into the world so that we may live through Him.* 10 *In this is love, not that we loved God, but that He loved us and sent His Son to be the propitiation for our sins.* 11 *Beloved, if God so loved us, we also ought to love one another.* 12 *No one has ever seen God; if we love one another, God remains in us, and His love is perfected in us.* 13 *By this we know that we remain in Him and He in us, because He has given to us of His Spirit.* 14 *We have seen and testify that the Father has sent the Son to be the Savior of the world.*

15 *Whoever confesses that Jesus is the Son of God, God remains in him, and he in God.* 16 *We have come to know and have believed the love which*

The Best Use of Life is Love

God has for us. God is love, and the one who remains in love remains in God, and God remains in him. **17** *By this, love is perfected with us, so that we may have confidence in the day of judgment; because as He is, we also are in this world.* **18** *There is no fear in love, but perfect love drives out fear, because fear involves punishment, and the one who fears is not perfected in love.* **19** *We love, because He first loved us.* **20** *If someone says, "I love God," and yet he hates his brother or sister, he is a liar; for the one who does not love his brother and sister whom he has seen, cannot love God, whom he has not seen.* **21** *And this commandment we have from Him, that the one who loves God must also love his brother and sister.*

We have started out on the Forty Days of Love program. I heard a definition of love which said, "Love is a temporary insanity cured by marriage." Tragically, for some that is their experience of love, but it is not supposed to be. But the question that should be asked when we speak of love is, "What love are we talking about?" We use the word "love" very loosely. I love Joan Neudorf's lemon meringue pies, and I love my wife, and I love my Spider and I love Stephen and Robyn who have been close friends for so many years, I love the work I have done for the Lord in the Philippines, and I love this church. Love has so many meanings that it is almost meaningless. There are so many different types and strengths of emotions that are covered by that word. Our New Testament is written in Greek and the ancient Greeks weren't as vague as we are when we talk of love. They had a number of words that are translated into English as "love." There is some value in looking at them briefly.

Love Type	Greek Word	Times noun is used
Natural affection	*Storge*	0
Friendship	*Philia*	1
Passion	*Epithymia*	38
Romantic love	*Eros*	0
Christian love	*Agape*	320

Table 8 Love words from the New Testament

Storge—Natural Affection

About twenty-three years ago my sister Jan had a bad nervous breakdown. Those of you who knew her could never imagine it, but she was a mess. In the midst of this she found out that she was pregnant. Not good timing! She resented that baby growing inside her, unplanned and years after her last child. She wanted to travel; she did not want to be tied down to an unplanned baby. But when Andrea was born those strong maternal bonds kicked in and of course her daughter was deeply loved. We know how strong family ties are. And ties to our country also were included in the meaning of this word and we are reminded of that this Anzac Day. This love is never based on worth but on natural affection, often towards the unworthy. The son may be an axe murderer, but his mother still loves him. But natural affection falls short of Christian love, and it is never used in the New Testament. But this love is presupposed for all people; only the absence is condemned—without natural affection (Rom 1:31). Why isn't it Christian love? Because there is nothing natural about the love of a holy God for his fallen and sinful creation.

Philia—Friendship

As I said, the Beasley's and the Stubbersfield's have been friends for a long time and we have gone through some very tough time together on both sides of the fence, but even unbelievers have friends. Jesus had said that our love has to transcend that. This is the word used of the love that God had for his son, a love based on equality and honor. You shouldn't be conceived without romantic love, and you can't be raised properly without natural affection but where is the survival value in friendship? As someone said, "It has no survival value: rather it is one of those things that give value to survival." Friendship is powerful, today on Anzac Day we are called to remember and honor our own fallen; many who gave their lives for friends.

This love falls short of Christian love and attitudes as the word is only used once and is of "friendship with the world" (Jas 4:4).

Epithymia—Passion

Have you ever had a passion in your life? It might have been for a person of the opposite sex and that is the usual meaning. The word can refer to passion towards your partner or just lust directed where it should not be. It is a word of mixed and sometimes positive meaning. It is used of Jesus for his desire to eat the Passover in Jerusalem (Luke 22:15), and Paul's longing to be with Christ. I was talking to my mum last week in her nursing home and again she spoke of her longing to be rid of this body and be with the Lord. There should be passion in our lives but correctly directed. Ula is passionate about art, Brendon and Katherine are passionate about baby Mia. Who would take these passions from them in the name of purifying themselves of all that is not of Christ?

What are you passionate about? I think there should be passion in our lives, but even when correctly directed this is not Christian love. None of the thirty-eight references in the New Testament are translated "love."

Eros—Romantic Love

Men, do you remember when you set your heart on winning your wife. Did you ever think in your mind "I am desperately in love with her, but she is going out with someone else, well that is okay if she marries him?" Eros, the scholars tell us is a love of the worthy, a love that desires to possess. It is directed to someone the beholder sees as beautiful.

This word isn't used in the New Testament, so it is not Christian love. But are we going to go to the recently married (or perhaps not so recently married) in the church and say, we are Baptists, we live by the scriptures, there is no Eros in the New Testament so you will have to cut it out. We would not be that silly but make no mistake, others have. In our spirituality we read the Song of Solomon as an allegory of Christ's love, but it is not its primary meaning. It tells us that romantic love at its best is a wonderful, pure love, lofty and ennobling. Rachel's bracelet is inscribed with "Song 4:9," which says, "You have enchanted my heart, my sister, *my* bride; You have enchanted my heart with a single *glance* of your eyes."

Agape—Christian Love

I have just touched on the words that were available to a writer at the time the New Testament was written, old words that describe emotions that are still fresh today. But some of you might be saying, "Ted; you have missed out a word, what about *agape*?" You can't have been in the church for years and not have heard the word *agape*. You don't have to be a Greek scholar to have stumbled across it, it is another love word. As we have seen, the writers of our New Testament had many other words available to them to describe Christian love but invariably they used none of them. They kept choosing the word *agape*. Just how common was this common New Testament word? In pre-Christian secular Greek writings, and there are a lot of them still existing, you cannot find this word at all, not once. You can find the verb *agapao* but not the noun *agape*. Then all of a sudden, this word just explodes among a small group of people called Christians. It is so common among them that in their writings it is virtually the only word they use. For all intents and purposes, they invented a new word. I am told that in German that if you want to draw attention to something you can invent a new word (read a few German theologians and you see it) and that ancient Greek was just the same.

So, a Greek living two thousand years ago, reading an epistle would say, "Hey what's this word, I have never heard it before." Something we just run over because we are familiar with it would have stopped him in his tracks. He would have had some idea where the meaning lay because he knew the verb, *agapao,* to prefer, but just what was Paul or John trying to say that there was no word in their vocabulary to use? It would have something to do with choosing.

Love Integrates My Life

A new word was needed that was free of the bad associations that other words had. We know that friendships can be as destructive as they are creative, that romantic love can easily turn to lust. The misguided love of country has seen the horrors of the world wars of the last century. We have a new word without a definition—there were no dictionaries. If you want to know what it means, one writer said go to the books that do not use the word, Mark, Acts and James, they show us what it is. There is an old saying, "It is better felt than telt." It has been said that if you want to understand Christian love, look at *eros*, a love of the worthy and a love that wants to possess, and then reverse the meaning. It is a love that is given without merit and a love that gives. It is a love that chooses what is best for the person loved. It is a love that chooses to love because God first loved us. It allows us to love the unlovely.

To be consumed with Christian love does not mean that we abandon every other love; rather it should integrate them into our lives in a more vibrant way. They cannot remain stable and produce what they promise without God's help. All the loves must submit to Christian love. Our friendships with other Christians are friendship firmly grounded in Christ and shared afflictions. When married life doesn't run smoothly, we don't run to the solicitor. We should have our reactions governed by mutual forgiveness because of the deep cost of the forgiving and choosing love of our savior.

Love Validates My Faith

The early church needed a new word because they had a new idea about the meaning of love. It was not a matter of saying one love was inferior, that romantic love is inferior to Christian love or friendship is inferior to Christian love. Can you imagine your life without these different loves? I don't think it would be worth living. They wanted a word that that demonstrated not the worth of one form of love over another, but the difference. It was the different love that the first Christians had that validated their faith. In 1 John chapter 4 we read:

> [19] We love, because He first loved us. [20] If someone says, "I love God," and yet he hates his brother or sister, he is a liar; for the one who does not love his brother and sister whom he has seen, cannot love God, whom he has not seen.

Love Compensates for My Sin

My favorite verse is probably 1 Peter 4:8, it is certainly the one that governs much of what I do. "[8]Above all, keep fervent in your love for one another, because love covers a multitude of sins." I am very conscious of failings in my life and nature. You find the same thought in I John 4:17-18, "[17] By this, love is perfected with us, so that we may have confidence in the day of judgment; because as He is, we also are in this world. [18] There is no fear in love, but perfect love drives out fear, because fear involves punishment, and the one who fears is not perfected in love."

Ah, you might say to me, "We are justified by faith and faith only." We can be so frightened of works but Christian faith without Christian action and Christian love is an aberration. The Epistle of James never mentions the word agape but if you want to see the quality of love that is meant by that word, look at James. If you want to be called a friend of God, it will only happen when your faith is bought to completion by works. Ted, you are changing the subject, you start talking about love and now you're talking about works. No! Christian love is work, or at least starts out that way. It is down to the central meaning of the word "choosing," Choosing to forgive and choosing to love.

Love Reverberates Forever

Out of all the things that consume us, only three go with us into the next world, 1 Corinthians 13:13 says, "And now faith, hope, and love abide, these three; and the greatest of these is love." You might say, I am a Baptist, and we hold correct doctrine and understanding about God, surely that must last forever? But you can hold these without love. 1 Corinthians 13:8 says, "Love never fails; but if *there are gifts of* prophecy, they will be done away with; if *there are* tongues, they will cease; if *there is* knowledge, it will be done away with." At the best we see and understand Christian things imperfectly, as Paul goes on to say, "For now we see in a mirror dimly, but then face to face; now I know in part, but then I will know fully, just as I also have been fully known. 13 But now faith, hope, *and* love remain, these three; but the greatest of these is love."

I have asked the question "What does it mean to love?" There are no new words for us but sadly for some in the Christian church it can be a new experience. Let it never be said of us. The challenge of these forty days is to love like we have never loved before. Well, yes, it is a good idea Ted, and the moment the Spirit moves me, I will do it. Make no mistake the Spirit can give great gifts of love for others and for the Lord himself. But for the rest of us, we can and must choose to love with Christian love. Even when this love is only partially mastered our natural affection, our friendships, our passions and even our intimacy take on a new depth.

Let us go forth and love and serve each other.

13

Giving the Shirt Off Your Back

Background

I AM RENOWN FOR my shirts. I was wearing a particularly colorful shirt that day. Why not, there is plenty of time in heaven to wear white.

Reading

Deuteronomy. 24:10–15, On treating the poor with dignity.

Text: Matthew 5:1-2, 38-40

Now when Jesus saw the crowds, He went up on the mountain; and after He sat down, His disciples came to Him. **2** *And He opened His mouth and began to teach them.* Part of what he taught them was:
38 *"You have heard that it was said, 'Eye for eye, and tooth for tooth.'* **39** *But I say to you, do not show opposition against an evil person; but whoever slaps you on your right cheek, turn the other toward him also.* **40** *And if anyone wants to sue you and take your tunic, let him have your cloak also.*

Brothers, bear with me while I stray from my topic for a while, sisters, tell me honestly, what do you think of this shirt? I bought it in Jakarta in

November when my daughter shouted her dear old mum and dad a trip to celebrate my sixtieth birthday. It is tailor made, lined inside, and cost all of $35.00. For $50 I could have had silk. When I was being measured up the first point of a sermon about a shirt dropped into my mind, but I didn't know where it was going to take me. The rest has been a hard slog.

You know, over these last forty years I have tried to cultivate in my own life the Christian graces as you have too. I could think of nothing better than for someone to say, "Ted Stubbersfield, he is a fine Christian man. Why he is so full of Christian grace that he would give you the very shirt off his back." To which some of the men are probably thinking, pity he cannot find anybody to take it! When my friend Dennis drove me to the airport that time I said, "Dennis, would you like me to bring you back a shirt? "That is last thing I want," he replied, "But Dennis, I have a lot of taste when it comes to shirts." He answered, "Yes Ted, and let me tell you, it is all bad!"

Be that as it may, over morning tea someone might come to me and say, "Ted, I like that shirt, can I have it?" (Jason is probably the only one it fits so I am fairly safe, though perhaps not.) "Yes of course and you can have the singlet as well." Now I must warn you that it is not a pretty site, but it is legal for the time being. After all, that is what our text says isn't it? Being generous? And if anyone wants to sue you and take your shirt, hand over your coat as well. Well, no it isn't. There is not necessarily any special grace and merit in generosity. We have witnessed it with the recent floods, yes, even those that do not know Christ can be generous, very generous indeed. Is the only message from this text that we should be no better than a good living unbeliever? Is the life set before us as we walk with Christ so easily achievable?

Evil People

No! Far from it. Our text is dealing with evil, not in an abstract concept, but with an evil person. "do not show opposition against an evil person." Jesus is not talking about the Devil who is always to be resisted, (James 4:7). Instead, the disciples of Jesus are commanded not to resist the evil man. Our text is dealing with revenge; our text is dealing with a lack of forgiveness. Our text is dealing with holding our own rights close to your heart. Our text is dealing with not finding Christ sufficient. It deals with having mastery over our own hearts, not only does it accept the injustice but gladly and voluntarily goes beyond what is demanded. I have not mastered my own heart.

Giving the Shirt Off Your Back

Some years ago, we had a dreadful time with the local council and the planning department. We kept winning matters that were so obviously correct. On the last meeting with the planner over that matter I was furious for all the heartache, frustration and delays he had caused. The mayor was there, Ray xxxx. He pulled me up and said, "Ted, you have to forgive this man." He was correct. I have not mastered my heart. It was wise advice.

Perhaps more importantly our text is about using God's word as the justification for sharing in the same sin as the evil person. How could we do that? He doesn't believe exactly what I believe, he has raised his hand against the Lord's anointed, mark those who cause divisions, I expect that we could write a long list of biblical excuses for not fully loving and fully accepting our brother and sister, let alone our enemy. But our Lord has placed in our heart the law of love not the sword of the judgement. If there are issues, then surely, we must love back in double measure.

Those who clung to an eye for an eye had to deal with Leviticus 19, 17 "You shall not hate your fellow countryman in your heart; you may certainly rebuke your neighbor, but you are not to incur sin because of him. 18 You shall not take vengeance, nor hold any grudge against the sons of your people, but you shall love your neighbor as yourself; I am the Lord." "Well Lord," the scribes and Pharisees said, "Your word did not define who my neighbor was, so I will decide who he is." If we have any resentment in our heart, we also like, the scribes and Pharisees, need to strive for a better righteousness

I have stood at the grave of Graham Staines and his boys; their martyrdom was one of the blackest deeds of humanity. That is what the Prime Minister of India said. We are not likely to meet such wickedness but make no mistake; evil people exist in our community, in varying degrees. You cannot get to my age without meeting evil people. I have had two lucky (as the world would say) brushes with IRA terrorism. While overt evil is out there, I expect that we will have to deal with its lesser forms. Betrayal of trust is one that I particularly have had to deal with. Our Lord very wisely commanded us to pray that we would be delivered from evil. No, this passage goes beyond the best that a good living unbeliever can muster. What our passage does not say is sweep evil under the carpet, it doesn't say your evil actions are now acceptable, it doesn't say it no longer matters, but it says expose it. But expose it on Christ's terms. Lord may we never be placed in a situation that Mrs. Staines was placed where she had to show what Christian grace is. She didn't seek vengeance but chose to forgive.

Sermons from a Potato Field

Back in 1972 I started my theological studies and I remember to this day my lecturer referring to our text as the "Impossible Commandment." Why is it impossible? Because men only wore two items of clothing, an outer garment, and an inner garment. If you did as Christ commanded, apart from the sandals you would be as you were born. The person who wanted the inner garment was going to be quite satisfied with that, why not just let well alone. It is like the man you strikes you on the right cheek, why give him the left cheek when he was satisfied with just the one punch? Why go the extra mile, these are fine words, but they are impossible to fulfil completely?

Why are the commands of Jesus so different to what the Father said to Moses, "An eye for an eye?" Did our loving and wise Heavenly Father get it wrong? No! It is the difference between Israel and the church. Israel was both a people of God and a state. Tied up with their command to be a holy and separate people of faith was the necessity to restrain wickedness. But our Lord's church should not be made up of people of divided attention. Last time I preached it was about the Baptist distinctive of separation of church and state. This is the outworking of the understanding of a people who find their completeness in Christ alone, to be free of their possessions, and their ego and bound to Christ alone.

"Jesus, how can you say that we must patiently endure the suffering caused by evil men? How can you say that suffering willingly endured is stronger than evil, that it can put a death to evil? Jesus, are we to be satisfied to let the evil man fall into your hands? Surely Jesus, these are nice words, but you are being impractical, don't you understand the harsh reality of this evil world. I know that you vanquished evil and triumphed over it on the cross, but the rules are different for me. I only want your victory but none of your suffering." Yet we are not blessed unless we participate in the cross.

Don't think I am saying anything goes. The strike to the cheek, give the shirt, go the extra mile are not all that serious. But there are some things in which we cannot yield. You need the wisdom that only the Spirit gives to discern what they are. But again, our actions must be different, not driven by anger but by concern for the other person. The disciple of Jesus who lives under the eye of his master always acts completely different from all other men.

Years ago, I heard a recording by a minister telling how he passed preaching class. The prospective pastors were set an assignment for the year, they had to collect newspaper clippings and file them under categories so they could use them as sermon illustrations. If you didn't make your catalogue of clippings, you could not pass and of course he didn't do it. But all was not lost. There was one other way of passing and that was to preach the final sermon for the class to critique. All through the course the four criteria for a good sermon had been drummed into them:

- It must have a text,
- It must have a single unifying theme,
- It must have achievable goals, and
- It should take 20 minutes.

Well, he memorized and preached the Sermon on the Mount. What have you got? No text, no unifying theme, impossible demands, and it only takes twelve minutes. Can you imagine if it actually had been Jesus? Next day he would have had to front the Dean. "Jesus, what are we going to do with you? For four years we have been trying to make you a fit person to pastor God's flock and still you can't preach properly. Whatever are we going to do with you? You ask too much of your people, no one can live at the heights you want them to reach. Fortunately, all is not lost; we could probably find a place for you as a hospital chaplain, only don't go and upset the system by praying for the sick."

Yes, I might give you the shirt off my back, but making progress as a fine gracious Christian man, that is another matter, the bar is too high for me ever to think I have made it. If you think you have made it, I tell you that you have only just started to scratch the surface and pray to God as he commanded us that we never encounter extreme evil and discover what a short distance we have travelled on the road to Christlikeness.

Evil Circumstances

Our reading spoke of another evil, the evil of circumstances for lack of a better word. And it speaks of another shirt, a shirt given as a guarantee for a loan. Imagine reaching such a low state that the only thing of value you have is your shirt. Imagine for a moment what it looked like, not as pretty as mine. His mum definitely did not have a Whirlpool or use Omo or Cuddly.[1] I suggest to you that it would have been a fairly disgusting garment by our standards, home spun, home woven and dirty. What could

---

1. Australian brands for a washing machine, laundry detergent and fabric softener.

it possibly be worth? To the man who has fallen on hard times it was worth everything. It kept him warm at night and he was to have it back.

In India such a man would not be treated with respect. It is karma; he had it coming because of sins in a former life. He is fortunate he did not come back as a cockroach. But Moses said treat him with respect and compassion, don't even go into his house to take the pledge, wait for him to bring it out.

In our text there was the command to give double what was demanded of us by compulsion. If we had read on to verse forty-two, we would have read "Give to the one who asks you, and do not turn away from the one who wants to borrow from you." Compulsion has gone and, in its place, a simple request. There is no talk now of taking a guarantee, just a simple command to give and to lend when you are asked, not double as with the evil person but simply meet the need. I said at the start that there is not necessarily any special grace in being generous and yet when it is driven by love of our neighbor and even our enemy it leads to a better righteousness. May we as a church be a people who become even more generous and be able to be more generous to those in need.

Conclusion

Would that life were just a matter of colored shirts and holidays but unfortunately all of us, or the people we love, will one day have to deal with either evil people or evil circumstances. May we be found to be a people who strive to reach the unreachable heights Christ has set for us. May we be a people who find their completeness in Christ, may we be a people who will give the shirts off our back. May we be a people who have risen to a better righteousness.

Dear Lord, deliver us from the evil of this fallen world.

14

Sermon Following the Boxing Day Tsunami

Background

THIS SERMON ON SEEKING the mercy of God in our circumstances seems appropriate as it was on the day, we learnt of the Boxing Day tsunami. I was not a member of the Tenthill Baptist Church at that time

First Text: Ezekiel 26:3-12

3 *Therefore this is what the Lord God says: 'Behold, I am against you, Tyre, and I will bring up many nations against you, as the sea brings up its waves.* 4 *They will destroy the walls of Tyre and tear down her towers; and I will sweep her debris away from her and make her a bare rock.* 5 *She will become a dry place for the spreading of nets in the midst of the sea, for I have spoken,' declares the Lord God; 'and she will become plunder for the nations.* 6 *Also her daughters who are on the mainland will be killed by the sword, and they will know that I am the Lord.'"*

7 *For the Lord God says this: "Behold, I am going to bring upon Tyre from the north Nebuchadnezzar king of Babylon, king of kings, with horses, chariots, cavalry, and a great army.* 8 *He will kill your daughters on the mainland with the sword; and he will make siege walls against you, pile up an assault ramp against you, and raise up a large shield against you.* 9 *And he*

will direct the blow of his battering rams against your walls, and he will tear down your towers with his axes. **10** *Because of the multitude of his horses, the dust raised by them will cover you; your walls will shake from the noise of cavalry, wagons, and chariots when he enters your gates as warriors enter a city that is breached.* **11** *With the hoofs of his horses he will trample all your streets. He will kill your people with the sword, and your strong pillars will go down to the ground.* **12** *Also they will take your riches as spoils and plunder your merchandise, tear down your walls and destroy your delightful houses, and throw your stones, your timbers, and your debris into the water.*

Second Text: Ezekiel 28 12–19

12 *"Son of man, take up a song of mourning over the king of Tyre and say to him, 'This is what the Lord God says:*
   "You had the seal of perfection,
   Full of wisdom and perfect in beauty.
   13 *You were in Eden, the garden of God;*
   Every precious stone was your covering:
   The ruby, the topaz and the diamond;
   The beryl, the onyx and the jasper;
   The lapis lazuli, the turquoise and the emerald;
   And the gold, the workmanship of your settings and sockets,
   Was in you.
   On the day that you were created
   They were prepared.
   14 *You were the anointed cherub who covers,*
   And I placed you there.
   You were on the holy mountain of God;
   You walked in the midst of the stones of fire.
   15 *You were blameless in your ways*
   From the day you were created
   Until unrighteousness was found in you.
   16 *By the abundance of your trade*
   You were internally filled with violence,
   And you sinned;
   Therefore I have cast you as profane
   From the mountain of God.
   And I have destroyed you, you covering cherub,

Sermon Following the Boxing Day Tsunami

From the midst of the stones of fire.
17 Your heart was haughty because of your beauty;
You corrupted your wisdom by reason of your splendor.
I threw you to the ground;
I put you before kings,
That they may see you.
18 By the multitude of your wrongdoings,
In the unrighteousness of your trade
You profaned your sanctuaries.
Therefore I have brought fire from the midst of you;
It has consumed you,
And I have turned you to ashes on the earth
In the eyes of all who see you.
19 All who know you among the peoples
Are appalled at you;
You have become terrified
And you will cease to be forever."""

Introduction

Christmas is now behind, and a new year is before us. 2004 has been written and for all of God's omnipotence he cannot change it. What resolutions did you make last New Year? Was it to lose weight? How long did you keep it?

What will 2005 hold, for good or ill. It is uncertain. On a personal level my own health has not been good, and I recently had a brain scan. Fortunately, they didn't find anything. On a local level there has been no flooding rains, Lord knows we need a wet season. On a national and international level, we are at war. I could not sleep on the night of 9/11 and came out and put the television on, only to see the Twin Towers fall. We have an enemy that does not wear a uniform and even lives in our midst. They hate us and what we represent with a passion that we cannot understand. They will gladly kill themselves in the process of killing us and do it with a prayer, thinking they are serving their god. Bali[1] or worse could easily be repeated on our shores

What will 2005 hold? Will it be the best year yet or our *anus horribilis*?

---

1. Nightclub bombings in Bali in 2002 killed 202 people, eighty-eight of whom were Australian. A further four Australians died in a 2005 attack.

Sermons from a Potato Field

Point 1. Our Text

We are not the first to live in perilous times. Our text is abbreviated, somewhere about 590 BC Ezekiel wrote three prophesies against Tyre. These were:
Chapter 26, A prophesy against Tyre,
Chapter 27, A lament for Tyre, and
Chapter 28, A prophesy against the king of Tyre.
All ending with the thought that God will bring Tyre to a horrible end.

These chapters contain strong words and in 28:11-17, Ezekiel sees behind the troubled times to spiritual reality behind the events. He starts to denounce the king of Tyre and then sees behind the king the one manipulating him, the god of this world. The times and places have changed many times, but the reality is still the same. There is an enemy of our soul and of God's kingdom that seeks our harm, the more so as his days draw short.

This is not the first prophesy about Tyre. Joel 3:5-6 is a prophesy of the destruction of Tyre because they sold the people of Jerusalem and Judea as slaves to the Greeks. Probably writing in nineth century BC and it is suggested in order of 820 BC

Jeremiah also wrote (25:22-29; 27:1-11) at somewhere around same time as Ezekiel, "This is what the Lord Almighty, the God of Israel says "[4] 'Order them *to go* to their masters, saying, 'This is what the Lord of armies, the God of Israel says: "This is what you shall say to your masters: [5] 'I have made the earth, mankind, and the animals which are on the face of the earth by My great power and by My outstretched arm, and I will give it to the one who is pleasing in My sight." The warning to Tyre was that, "If I am going to judge Jerusalem do you think you will go unpunished?"

Here is the point I could wax lyrical about, our Lord holds the times and destiny of the forces on mankind in his hand even in the most turbulent of times. Now there is nothing that is going to take him by surprise. Just as he had spoken about Tyre with the sure word of prophesy that must surely come to pass, our Lord could speak about your destiny and mine 250 years in advance just as easily as he can three years in advance. Just as Ezekiel seems to be saying, the year 589 BC was all mapped out and God is still on the throne so is 2005. But that is not what I see in this passage

From Ezekiel 29:17-20 we see it didn't happen:

> [17] Now in the twenty-seventh year, in the first month, on the first of the month, the word of the Lord came to me, saying, [18] "Son of man, Nebuchadnezzar king of Babylon made his army labor hard

Sermon Following the Boxing Day Tsunami

against Tyre; every head had a bald spot, and every shoulder was rubbed raw. But he and his army acquired no wages from Tyre for the labor that he had performed against it." **19** Therefore this is what the Lord God says: "Behold, I am going to give the land of Egypt to Nebuchadnezzar king of Babylon. And he will carry off her wealth and capture her spoils and seize her plunder; and it will be wages for his army. **20** I have given him the land of Egypt for his labor which he performed, because they acted for Me," declares the Lord God."

How can we know when a message has not been spoken by the Lord? If what a prophet proclaims in the name of the Lord does not take place or come true, that is the message the Lord has not spoken. "**22** When the prophet speaks in the name of the Lord, and the thing does not happen or come *true*, that is the thing which the Lord has not spoken. The prophet has spoken it presumptuously; you are not to be afraid of him" (Deut 18:22). Are we going to say that of Jeremiah and Ezekiel? You would be gamer than me.

Point 2. God Is Merciful

Do we say it of Jonah? "Yet forty days and Nineveh shall perish." There was no word of hope, only the sure word of prophesy again but the king dared to ask (4:9) "Who knows, God may turn and relent, and turn from His burning anger so that we will not perish." He asks the deepest of questions, can God change his mind? For the king who believed the message, God did change his mind and Jonah was furious (4:2), "I knew that You are a gracious and compassionate God, slow to anger and abundant in mercy, and One who relents of disaster."

What did God say to Jonah to justify his actions? "Should I not also have compassion on Nineveh, the great city in which there are more than 120,000 people, who do not know *the difference* between their right hand and their left, *as well as* many animals?" Aren't we as God's deeply loved children dearer to him than these Ninevites who did not know the law? Hasn't our repentance been deeper? Aren't we of more value than many head of cattle? Is he more likely to listen to them or you? If God can choose to re-write the history of Nineveh and Tyre, then 2005 has not been written for us or our nation. The only thing certain about next year is that there is one thing stronger than God's will and that is his love and compassion for you and for the whole community of faith and also for his creation

Christianity does not know blind acceptance of the present reality. We do not shrug our shoulders and say, "It is God's will." But we ask, "Why" and of change we say, "Why not?"

Application

In my own church I hear prayers to change the reality of those in the church and wider community. I also see some remarkable answers to prayer, but I do not hear prayers for the safety of our country, safety of our peacekeepers, and good government by our politicians or to change the evils in our community (may God bless Mr. Abbot[2] for his stance on abortion.) Much world trouble is centered on Jerusalem, Psalm 122:6 commands us to pray for its peace.

Emphasis on deeper spiritual life can be counterproductive if it only results in navel gazing and is not directed outwards to our community. I expect this church has no problem looking to God to change his mind about our local reality. You pray for rain, you pray for those who are sick, you pray for loved ones who are not converted but as a community do you ask God to change the reality of our nation. and this troubled world.

What good will it do? James 5:16 says, "A prayer of a righteous person, when it is brought about, can accomplish much." There are more people in church each Sunday than attend Australian Rules football for a complete season. If God is good to his word, it will do much.

Who can tell if God will turn and repent and turn away from his fierce anger?

---

2. Our Prime Minister at the time.

15

Reflections on the Death of a Young Man

Background

THIS SERMON WAS PREACHED following the tragic death of a young Christian father who lived near the church. He had two aunties who are members of our church. The sermon was preached just after Australia Day, the national celebration of the arrival in Australia of the first fleet with convict settlers on January the twenty-sixth, 1788. The text used is the same one used by the chaplain to the settlement on the first church service in our land.

Text: Psalm 116:12-13

12 What shall I repay to the Lord
For all His benefits to me?
13 I will lift up the cup of salvation,
And call upon the name of the Lord.

On Thursday night Reg rang me and said, "Ted, what is your Bible reading?" "What do you want that for Reg?" "You are preaching Sunday." I hate to say, I had mislaid my roster, so I hurriedly prepared one in my mind on Thursday night, but the events of that night quickly overtook us, and that sermon will be for another day, but not my text. "Today I must talk to you as mortals, yet immortals."

Psalm 116:12–13 says, "What shall I repay to the Lord for all His benefits to me? [13] I will lift up the cup of salvation and call upon the name of the Lord." On the twenty-sixth at Lake Apex Café, there was an Australia Day function where our sister Ula was honored with the Senior Cultural Award. As well a number of new Australians received citizenship certificates. I noticed that most of these new citizens were Sudanese. When you think of the hell hole that the Sudan is, (and hell hole is probably the best word to describe that country because such misery can only come from the pit of Hell,) Australia must surely have looked like Utopia. It wasn't always like this. Consider the lot of the first "boat people."

Under a large gum tree on the shores of Sydney Cove on the first Sunday after the fleet landed, the Reverend Richard Johnston held our nation's first church service. His text that day is the same as mine "What shall I render unto the Lord for all his benefits towards me. I will take up the cup of salvation and call upon the name of the Lord." One of the officers reported, "We had a very good sermon . . . The behavior of the convicts was regular and attentive." And well it might be, the Reverent Johnson had, after all, a captive audience. You see, church attendance was compulsory as Governor Philip wanted to improve their morals; failure to attend meant a two-pound deduction in the meagre rations for the week. There were armed marines to ensure that the thousand or so people stayed attentive.

What do you think went through their minds that Sunday morning? I don't think that there would have been too many receptive hearts among them. What shall I render unto the Lord for all his benefits towards me, what a load of old rubbish? For ten months we have been cramped up on those ships and have buried forty at sea along way. They were the lucky ones. England has rejected us and cast us off and sent us to this hell hole, hot when it should be cold, trees and landscaping we don't recognize, strange animals, no houses, no roads, no fields, and if we stray from the camp we will probably be speared by a savage. Nothing will ever be the same again. Here they will work us till we drop, and we will never see home or loved ones again. Now on our only day off we have to come and listen to this old claptrap. What shall I render unto the Lord for all his benefits towards me? I would like to see just some of that goodness he was waffling on about. There will be no gentleness and peace for us.

Reflections on the Death of a Young Man

Who under that blazing sun would have had the vision to see Australia as it is today, a land where people would risk life and limb and cross any ocean to reach? Which of them, especially when the early crops failed and they had a pain in their belly from hunger, would have seen the prosperity and freedom ahead? By 1830, after receiving their ticket of leave the convict's labor would be in high demand and the wages and conditions better than in England or Ireland. They could raise a family and be beholding to no one. Many would own their own land. As more and more letters came back to England saying that they were not broken by the system and were prospering, the word would come back from London, make the conditions harder. Yet in 1840 the British home secretary would complain "that most English criminals now thought of transportation as a passport to opportunity and even wealth." Who would have imagined that for a further seventeen years after the commencement of the gold rushes that Britain would be sending its castoffs free of charge to our shore?

Would one of them there under that gum tree, guard, or convict, had the vision to look twenty, thirty, forty years ahead to see that heartache and oppression for most would ease or even cease. To be able to look beyond the present day is a great gift and the Reverend Johnston urged them to seek this gift. But a vision that spans even 200 years is not enough. It must span eternity. In the first piece of Christian literature written in Australia, Reverend Johnston wrote of what he said to these men, "I do not address you as churchmen or dissenters, Roman Catholics, or protestants, as Jews or Gentiles... But I speak to you as mortals and yet immortals... The gospel proposes a free and gracious pardon to the guilty, cleansing to the polluted, healing to the sick, happiness to the miserable and even life for the dead." My assessment of what went through their minds was not fanciful and had to be near the mark. This godly minister had very few results despite his tireless labors. A ticket of leave from the governor was of more value than a pardon from their maker. They would only view themselves as mortals.

We can't know the sadness, hardship, and brutality that our founding fathers endured, but most of us here are old enough to have shaken off the naivety of childhood and youth. We know that God has blessed us with a wonderful land, but we have learned that it is not Utopia. Last week we had news that my sister's cancer treatment had not been successful and on Friday we were confronted with the possibility that Rachel's old enemy, cancer, had reoccurred. Fortunately for Rachel it was some other problem and I expect it is easily fixed, but Jan's will not go away.

Sermons from a Potato Field

Rachel and I had dinner with Wilf and Joan last week and as they told us about their life, we had an insight into the anxiety and sorrow that had come across their threshold. Yet, as I look around me, I do not see any shackles, no shirts with the broad arrow, not even one-armed guard to force us into this chapel and pay attention, though possibly some of us could do with a two-pound deduction to our rations. We are here because we choose to be here despite the adverse circumstances of our life. We, all like Reverend Johnson, have the same question on our heart, "What shall I render unto the Lord for all his benefits towards me?"

Yet, in the stillness, if we are completely honest, there are times when the words, "What shall I render unto the Lord for all his benefits towards me," can ring so hollow. When Rachel was given up for dead, I knew I would receive grace, but I did not want grace I wanted my wife safe and well! And we find this same thought had troubled the psalmist. Our Psalm is a bit of a problem. One writer said, "Some commentators seem to feel that the logical development of thought is not as carefully carried through as it might be." This is probably why many translations including the Septuagint the ancient Greek translation and the Vulgate, the Latin translation, and many more split Psalm 116 into two separate Psalms. Verses one to nine show thanksgiving to a God who preserves the simple, who is merciful and delivers from every problem. That is how we want our life and our God to be; easy, understandable, and needing no faith. The other half, verses ten to nineteen, deals with rash things the psalmist had said publicly and with that, the rash things he has thought in the silence of his mind. He has obviously had to deal with a death, but as he reflected upon it, it had brought with it a new understanding of who he is and his godly heritage. Behind it is frustration with men and quite possibly with God himself. But he has worked through it. He has realized that there is great benefit in serving God and now he will publicly pay his vow.

But there are not two separate psalms with simple and separate thoughts and experiences. The Hebrew text does not have a break. Exultation, disappointment, and frustration are all from the same Psalm and try as we would to live only in the first half, sooner or later, for most of us at least, we have to live and believe both sides of the coin together.

I find myself often being drawn to the words in this funny old Gadsby's hymnbook, there is one hymn in particular, which I often reflect on. It was written by Richard Burnham a Baptist pastor in Soho London, at about the same time that Rev. Johnston was preaching at Sydney Cove. It starts:

Reflections on the Death of a Young Man

God shall alone the refuge be, and comfort of my mind;
too wise to be mistaken, he, too good to be unkind.

His hymn progresses to the coming of a day when we will no longer be asked to hold this claim of God's goodness and wisdom by faith in tension with what our heart might tell us. There is coming a great day of celebration where, in the words of the last verse:

Hereafter he will make me know, and I shall surely find.
He was too wise to err, and o, too good to be unkind.

Rachel is finally going to take out Australian citizenship so that immigration will no longer threaten to deport her when she tries to enter Australia with an expired visa. She will have dual citizenship. But you know, we all beat her to it, we all have dual citizenship, and that citizenship is from above. But it can be very difficult to live in two kingdoms at once and have a vision that spans across them both. One of my favorite hymns is, I understand, in the top ten favorite hymns in the UK. And that is the soldier's hymn, *I Vow to thee, my Country*. Its first verse sings of the deep love that a person may have for his country which can equally be applied to a family. The last line of its second verse moves me profoundly when I hear it sung

And there's another country, I've heard of long ago—
Most dear to them that love her, most great to them that know;
We may not count her armies, we may not see her king;
Her fortress is a faithful heart, her pride is suffering;
And soul by soul and silently her shining bounds increase,
And her ways are ways of gentleness, and all her paths are peace.

There is nothing we can render for his benefits towards us, though as one commentator said, "We do what we can," but our Lord only asks that we take up the cup of his salvation; we get our visa in order and call upon his name. To all who do that, he will ensure that we will finally see that great day when gentleness and peace will be seen without measure on this troubled earth.

The Lord bless you and keep you; the Lord make his face to shine upon you and be gracious unto you; the Lord lift up his countenance upon you and give you peace. Amen.

16

The Lying Baptists

Background

THE CHURCH WAS BEING divided following a disastrous pastorate. I also was considering if my time at Toowoomba Assembly of God was coming to a close. The sermon deals with the subject of whether the things that divide us are stronger than the things that unite us. Many people hugged me as I left the pulpit. As for me, I decided they were stronger and only eventually left with a letter of recommendation to Tenthill Baptist Church after my wife's health deteriorated and it was becoming impossible for her to make the journey.

Text: Jeremiah 38:23-28.

23 They are also going to bring out all your wives and your sons to the Chaldeans, and you yourself will not escape from their hand, but will be seized by the hand of the king of Babylon, and this city will be burned with fire."

24 Then Zedekiah said to Jeremiah, "Let no one know about these words, and you will not die. 25 But if the officials hear that I have talked with you and come to you and say to you, 'Tell us now what you said to the king and what the king said to you; do not hide it from us and we will not put you to death,' 26 then you are to say to them, 'I was presenting my plea before the

The Lying Baptists

king, not to make me return to the house of Jonathan to die there.'" **27** *Then all the officials came to Jeremiah and questioned him. So he reported to them in accordance with all these words which the king had commanded; and they stopped speaking with him, since the conversation had not been overheard.* **28** *So Jeremiah stayed in the courtyard of the guard until the day that Jerusalem was captured.*

Context

Under godly Josiah, Judah had turned from worshiping foreign gods but on his death, they quickly reverted to their old ways. Jeremiah was called by God to prophesy to the nation the consequences of abandoning the God of their forefathers. He fell afoul of the governing authorities and was kept in appalling conditions. With the army of Babylon at the gate, the message of the fall of Jerusalem would have seen him killed.

Introduction. The Lying Baptists

Jack Hoad, in his book *The Baptist* lists the main Baptist groups as Particular, General and Southern. But there are numerous splinter groups among the Baptists, this includes:

- Seven day,
- Free will, and
- New connection.

But in my reading, I also found the "Lying Baptists." Now perhaps you can think of a few individuals, but not of a whole church. Let me tell you a story. In 1804, the Long Run Baptist Church in frontier Kentucky were holding a "log rolling," that is a big church picnic with a purpose, to build a home. Someone suggested holding a debate. Imagine your stockade is attacked by Indians. You hide your four children and then the stockade is breached, and three children are killed. Then the Indians sue for peace, but before you smoke the peace pipe they ask, "Are there any more children?" How do you reply? Do you tell the truth which the Baptist moral code demanded, or do you beg for mercy which you know you will not receive, or do you tell a lie? Do you let the last words on your lips before you stand before your Judge be a lie?

The church split. The Long Run Baptist Association became known as the "Truthful Baptists," they were the legitimate church, they would tell the truth despite the consequences. The others said they would lie to protect their last child. They moved twenty miles away and started a new church, the Flat Rock Baptist Church and were known as the "Lying Baptists." It would be interesting to have a show of hands to see if this is a gathering of Truthful or Lying Baptists. But the last thing we need is Tenthill Baptists going down in church history for the wrong reasons.

Point 1. We Are Still Faced With Questions About the Basis of Fellowship

The questions we face are not the same. Imagine a government official comes on to property with satellite photo to put meters on all your bores, and he says, "Do you have any more bores?" What do you say about the one under the tree that doesn't show up? Do you tell a lie? The question that day in 1804 was not a hypothetical question. The site of the log rolling was where Abe Lincoln's grandfather was killed by Indians, his father barely escaped. Joseph Fletcher, a theologian in the sixty's, used this example in arguments to support *Situation Ethics*. That is where, it is argued, there is no absolute right or wrong. But that is not where we are headed today.

Consider how quickly a day that had started so well in sweet fellowship and unity of purpose ended in bitterness, division and name calling. This is at the forefront of my mind as I make the decision this week, whether to leave my church of many years, a church I have loved and move 20 miles and perhaps even join with you.

An old founding member of my own church wrote "I remember the second cottage meeting I went to," she said. "My husband and I travelled twelve miles to it in a sulky after we'd been harvesting all day and cooking for thirteen men. We were determined not to miss it." She went on, "In the winter we wrapped hot bricks to keep our feet warm in the sulky. The warmth would last only till we got to the meeting. Coming home it was a case of cold feet, but hearts warm with the blessing of the Lord." I felt like this many times but now I find reasons not to attend.

I look for the church I love and can only see shadows. I must answer the questions:

- What is covered by charity? Love covers a multitude,

The Lying Baptists

- How much do you put up with?
- What is not negotiable? and
- Out of what I think is important, what really is important?

Should the Long Run Baptist Church have been split?

Point 2. Our Pastors Are Only Human

Wouldn't we love to have a pastor that can hear from God like Jeremiah? A pastor who could stand in pulpit and encourage us to holy living and denounce sin?

"Friend deceives friend, and no one speaks the truth,
They have taught their tongues to lie; they weary themselves with sinning" (9:5).

Oops

Or would we be happy to have him? Look, he tells lies, not to save his children's life but his own. How would even the Lying Baptists judge that? The problem with Jeremiah was that he was human, just like father Abraham was human and was caught out lying on two occasions.

The nation was in peril, the Babylonians were at the gate. There was a lot of prophesying to do, perhaps Jeremiah was thinking, "Who will do it if I don't. It is just a little lie." When Elisha was in peril (2 Kings 6) he asked the Lord to open this servant's eyes. What did he see? Chariots of fire! Where were those chariots now? Who needs chariots of fire when a little lie will achieve the same effect?

My own church was founded in 1927. The congregation and elders rebelled when the founding evangelist Van Eyk got too friendly with the leader's daughter. Barry Chant, in his history of the Pentecostal Church in Australia, describes what happened, "It became increasingly obvious that this was more than a platonic relationship. Christians who at first sought to believe only the best soon found it impossible to believe anything but the worst. Slowly, their doubts became fears and fears became anger." He was married, the church split on the basis of truth verses anointing and truth verses authority. The details are found in a number of sources. My own church was founded on the basis that truth and righteousness outweighs any charismatic gifting.

The problem with my ministers is that they are human like me. To my knowledge no one in my church is telling lies. No one is in immoral relationships. That would make the decision easy. Their failing is that they are human. This demands charity, not judgement from me as I decide what to do. They see preaching and the sacraments differently to me. Even if I am right, and they are wrong, it is not just enough to be right.

Point 3. Long Term Spirituality Under Stress Is Difficult

Poor Jeremiah, he had been beaten down by a long time in prison. He was rescued from a dry cistern where he was expected to die. It all has an effect, no matter how spiritual you are.

Dietrich Bonhoeffer was a director of a seminary of the anti-Hitler Confessing Church in Germany. In his book, *Letters and Papers from Prison* we see this process taking place. He was thrown into a German prison in April 1943 and was hung two years later for his involvement in a plot to assassinate Hitler. Initially all is well, after 12 days he says, "Up to now cells on each side of me have been occupied almost solely by fettered men awaiting death . . . During this time, I have been preserved from any serious spiritual trial." By the end of 1943 he wrote, "Things here are [so] revolting, that my grim experiences often pursue me into the night and that I can shake them off only by reciting one hymn after another, and that I am apt to wake up with a sigh rather than a hymn of praise to God." Despite an outward show of spiritual strength, the horrors of that prison day after day bore down upon him and a poem, *Who am I*, wrote of his true struggle and sense of hypocrisy:

> Restless and longing and sick, like a bird in a cage,
> Struggling for breath, as though hands were compressing my throat.
> Weary and empty at praying, at thinking, at making,
> Faint, and ready to say farewell to it all.

It is hard to have a constant confession over a long time of stress or disappointment. It is reported that a dour Scotsman who had a legalistic attitude to the Sabbath was confronted with the words of Jesus that the Sabbath was made for man. "Ah yes," he replied, "But only in a weaker moment." We all have weaker moments. If great men experience this problem how much more will we. It clouds your judgement to a greater or lesser degree. I once had strong words with a minister, me who would run a mile rather than have a confrontation. The Bible says be angry and sin not and

The Lying Baptists

I was angry. Being angry is so foreign to me that I recoil from it. I do not know if I crossed from righteous indignation to sin and if so by how much.

The problem is that we are like our pastors, we are human with all the frailties that come with our humanity. Pastors need the same charity dealing with us as we do with them.

Conclusion

Today I have broken the cardinal sin in preaching; I have preached to an individual; I have preached to myself. I should have sought God more earnestly for a message for you. I have only posed questions and given no answers but perhaps there were some pointers. If I knew the answers, I wouldn't have to be asking the questions. Sometimes I think there isn't a hard and fast answer.

What is important is the church. It is not the minister's church, and it is not the congregation's church, but it is Christ's church. The decision I must make is what is best for his church and will strengthen his body

Pray for us over the coming week.

17

My Cup Does Not Overflow

Background

Pastor Alan Gordon, the Intentional Interim Pastor[1] at the time, held a series of classes for the lay workers in the Tenthill Baptist Church to assist them in preparing messages. This sermon was prepared as an exercise as part of this course. It was actually delivered in a small church in the Philippines. It was met with tears by a number of the elderly.

Text: Psalm 23

¹ *The Lord* is my shepherd,
   I will not be in need.
   ² *He lets me lie down in green pastures;*
   He leads me beside quiet waters.
   ³ *He restores my soul;*
   He guides me in the paths of righteousness
   For the sake of His name.
   ⁴ *Even though I walk through the valley of the shadow of death,*

---

1. An Intentional Interim Pastor is one that is trained in the process of bringing healing to churches that were damaged and, in the process, damaged others. It is normally about eighteen months long and is intended to produce a church that can be handed on whole to the next pastor.

My Cup Does Not Overflow

I fear no evil, for You are with me;
Your rod and Your staff, they comfort me.
⁵ You prepare a table before me in the presence of my enemies;
You have anointed my head with oil;
My cup overflows.
⁶ Certainly goodness and faithfulness will follow me all the days of my life,
And my dwelling will be in the house of the Lord forever.

Introduction

The Twenty-third Psalm is well known to Australians as it is frequently sung at funerals. This great psalm about living is seldom sung during a normal worship service. But when should we sing this psalm, and to answer this I am asking, "When did David sing it?"

Point 1. The Young David

I have read a number of Lutheran theological books and they frequently refer to the young Luther and the old Luther, the young visionary working out his theology as he dealt with different crises and the old man, theology sorted but disillusioned in many ways. I remember when I had fire but not much theology, but now I have theology but not much fire. You older hearers have all changed, young people you will change too. Over his life David changed also. Whose words are these; are we looking at the young man or the old?

The Chinese curse is, "May you live in interesting times." It was David's misfortune (or fortune) to live in interesting times. If Saul was a better king and a better man, if the Philistines were not so active, we probably would not have heard of a person called David. This boy, courageous and with a heart after God would have spent his life looking at the back end of stupid sheep and his story lost in the dust of time. Perhaps if he was living in Tenthill in Queensland (my church) not Bethlehem, he may have spent his life moving irrigation pipes or in the cabin of the tractor. If he lived in Macawayan he would have been driving trucks, building houses, or making fine jewelry. He would have had plenty of time to think about his maker and himself. Time to think great thoughts like *The Lord is my shepherd I'll not want*.

Have you ever considered what a blessing it is to live an ordinary life in ordinary days? A mad king, soothed only by music would take the musician David from the flock, and a war would turn him from a shepherd into a man of blood.

He guides me in the paths of righteousness for the sake of His name. Leading his sheep, he would never have to plumb the depth of the depravity that existed in his heart. When the prophet Nathan came before him and described in a parable the terrible actions of a certain rich man in his kingdom, David said this man is not worthy of living (2 Sam 12:5), and Nathan said, "You are the man." Adultery and murder would stain his hands and he could no longer see it.

What will you do tomorrow? For most of us, it will be much the same as the day before, and the year before and the year before that. Just like young David, take the sheep out, take the sheep in, and dealing with the crises as they arise one by one. How wonderful it is to be able to spend our time looking outward at the shepherd of our soul than being forced to confront the hidden darkness. The ordinary life is a blessing beyond measure.

Point 2. The Old David

Though I walk through the valley of the shadow of death I fear no evil. The young David could face down and kill a bear and take a lamb from its mouth, he could kill a lion, he could slay Goliath. This was one brave man. But how that changed over time. Look at 1 Samuel 21:12–15, [12] "David took these words to heart and greatly feared Achish king of Gath. [13] So he disguised his sanity *while* in their sight and acted insanely in their custody, and he scribbled on the doors of the gate, and drooled on his beard. [14] Then Achish said to his servants, 'Look, you see the man is behaving like an insane person. Why do you bring him to me? [15] Do I lack insane people, that you have brought this one to behave like an insane person in my presence? Shall this one come into my house?'"

How difficult it is to withstand constant pressure; it grinds down the most spiritual. In my own home region, we do not fight men but almost God himself because of a severe drought, ten years without seasonal rain. Good farmers and good people may lose their farms and their incomes. One bad season or even two you can bear financially and emotionally but not ten. Many are anxious at home. What troubles afflict you here? Do you get depressed, even despair? It may not be because you lack faith, remember that you are human and no matter how willing the spirit is the flesh still remains weak. Go to the Lord and ask him to remember you are but dust, to ease the burden. He did for David, but it was all in the course of time.

A Digression

Let me digress from my message. I want to say something to those who are asking whether they have a call on their life. How do you think David slept at night? With one eye open? What visions came to his mind when dreams finally came? How many times must David have wished Samuel had never anointed him as king? How many times would he have given up his calling as a shepherd to the nation and returned to the sheep just to have a good night's sleep, to not have blood on his hands, to have peace in his family? How many times would the call not be viewed as blessing but a burden too heavy for one man to carry. I saw brother Noe[2] at such a time and I resolved as much as the Lord permits, I would help to ease that burden.

Do you think the Lord is calling you to be a shepherd to his flock? Think long and hard and pray carefully before you give up the ordinary life God has blessed you with. If the calling is real, he will not let you go, there will be no fleeing from it. If you accept the call, at times the burden will be so deep because it asks everything of you, your life, and your all. Someone who has not passed through it cannot understand it. But because God loves the sheep deeply, he gives them shepherds to lead them and bear their burdens, tend their wounds. Because he loves the sheep, he will make you able to bear the burden

Now Let Us Return to Our Psalm

Your rod and Your staff, they comfort me. Even when things seemed to be going right and he was finally king, David could not escape that his own power was not enough and God's power at times could not be seen. After the murder of Abner by his general Joab he said in 2 Samuel 3 38–39, **8** Then the king said to his servants, "Do you not know that a leader and a great man has fallen in Israel this day? **39** And I am weak today, though anointed king; and these men, the sons of Zeruiah, are too difficult for me. May the Lord repay the evildoer in proportion to his evil." Lord why don't

---

2. Noe Galzote, my friend in the Philippines.

you just deal with them and be quick about it. In Joab's case the matter was not resolved until after David died. Justice will not be denied forever.

Certainly goodness and faithfulness will follow me all the days of my life. David you barely knew the meaning of the words once you left the sheep.

> 1 Samuel 27. **8** *Now David and his men went up and attacked the Geshurites, the Girzites, and the Amalekites; for they were the inhabitants of the land from ancient times, as you come to Shur even as far as the land of Egypt.* **9** *David attacked the land and did not leave a man or a woman alive, and he took the sheep, the cattle, the donkeys, the camels, and the clothing. Then he returned and came to Achish.* **10** *Now Achish said, Where did you carry out an attack today?" And David said, "Against the Negev of Judah, against the Negev of the Jerahmeelites, and against the Negev of the Kenites."* **11** *And David did not leave a man or a woman alive to bring to Gath, saying, "Otherwise they will tell about us, saying, 'This is what David has done.*

David, how many of them cried to you for mercy? Are you merciful? None of us here have the weighty matters of state to deal with; none of us have to deal with open warfare. Mercy should not be the duty of any of us here but our nature.

As a young man he sang, *And my dwelling will be in the house of the Lord* forever. As an older man, when the prophet confronted him, he said in Psalm 51:11 and 12, *Do not cast me away from Your presence, and do not take Your Holy Spirit from me. Restore to me the joy of Your salvation, and sustain me with a willing spirit.* Perhaps here he pondered *where can I flee from your presence.* Perhaps here he longed for *the wings of a dove, to fly away and be at rest.* David would later no longer want to flee but to build the temple. The difference is repentance. Never lose sight of this church being a forgiven and forgiving community.

Conclusion

What has been your experience between when you walked as a youth with the Lord and now as older men and women? If you have been granted the blessing of an ordinary life, to have been *led beside still waters* it may well be the life of great blessing. Perhaps *your cup still overflows.*

Are you now old and life has been hard for you? Could you say, "I wish it had always been like the Psalm of David's but honestly it wasn't always."

My Cup Does Not Overflow

Do you look back and say, there are things I do not understand and wished they were different? Can you not still say "The Lord has been a good shepherd to me even though my cup now does not overflow?"

Have things changed to your youth? Does the shepherd of your soul seem far away? Remember the words *you are with me.* The young shepherd knew it, the king knew it, "^{8} If I ascend to heaven, You are there; if I make my bed in Sheol, behold, You are there.^{9} If I take up the wings of the dawn, If I dwell in the remotest part of the sea,^{10} Even there Your hand will lead me, And Your right hand will take hold of me.^{11} If I say, "Surely the darkness will overwhelm me, And the light around me will be night,"^{12} Even darkness is not dark to You, And the night is as bright as the day. Darkness and light are alike to You."

He *prepares a table for you in the presence of your enemies,* even when that enemy seems to be the Lord himself. He longs to *anoint your head with oil,* just as the father of the prodigal would have anointed his son. He wants to fill your cup to overflowing. When can we sing this psalm? Funerals are great, but not at mine. This is a psalm for the living, for those who know God and those who have known him and those who want to know him again.

18

Unswearing an Oath of Allegiance

Background

"Unswearing an Oath of Allegiance" is a communion address, not a sermon. It was prompted after visiting the Church of England in Fressingfield, Suffolk, UK and hearing the story of Archbishop Sancroft. A close friend, David Steere was the pastor of the Baptist Church in that village.

Address

The word used by theologians for those two special rites of the church, Baptism and the Lord's Supper is "Sacraments." Now traditionally, Baptists have resisted using that word because there were so many abuses against them because of our stance on baptism. Fortunately, we Australian Baptists have been largely free of the blood and smoke that had been the lot of our European brothers and sisters. We needn't be afraid of this word because it is a great word and full of meaning.

The word is Latin; it is not a Biblical term. *Sacramentum* can be found in the Vulgate in Ephesians 5:32 where it is used to describe something that was hidden but is now revealed. But really, its use with baptism and communion is with something visible but in which something is hidden. But why did the early church choose this word?

Unswearing an Oath of Allegiance

The *Sacramentum* was the first oath of a Roman Legionnaire. We do not know the exact words, but Livy said it was the "oath of allegiance administered to them by the tribunes, but they used to pledge each other not to quit the force by flight, or in consequence of fear, and not to leave the ranks except to seek a weapon, strike a foe, or save a comrade."

Think of those words "Pledge each other not to quit the force by flight, or in consequence of fear and not to leave the ranks." Doesn't this oath so closely resemble the pledge we made to our Lord through baptism?

Archbishop Sancroft 1617–1693

Sermons from a Potato Field

Graeme[1] should have seen this painting when he visited Pastor Steere in Fressingfield in Suffolk. The painting is of Archbishop William Sancroft (born 1617) who is buried in that small churchyard. Now, Archbishops of Canterbury are buried in Canterbury not small churchyards. Archbishop Sancroft was the head of the Anglican Church when James II was removed, and William and Mary become the rulers of the UK. You see the archbishop had sworn an oath of allegiance to King James 2nd who was still alive. He argued, "How can I unswear an oath of allegiance." The new king respected his position and allowed him to return home and retire in peace. The archbishop would not unswear his oath to a King of England but look around us to seats empty of people who have unsworn an oath of allegiance to the King of the Universe.

There was another and earlier meaning of the word *Sacramentum*. Solicitors have not changed from the days when Romans went to litigation with each other. They want to know that they will be paid. A deposit was placed in the temple to say that they can pay in full. That deposit was called a *sacramentum*.

We have only been given a down payment on the promised eternal life but like the funds deposited in the temple; our Lord says that contrary to our lack of faithfulness, he can pay in full. When our Lord instituted communion there was a promise that we would eat with him in his kingdom. He can be trusted completely with his promises to us.

---

1. One of our elders.

19

Psalm 85

Reading

Psalm 85.

Text: Psalm 85:10

Graciousness and truth have met together;
Righteousness and peace have kissed each other.

Back in 1974 I first started to court my wife. Now I do not know if I should be saying this from the pulpit, but I remember the first time I kissed my wife, it was very nice. Rachel has promised me that, if I behave myself and am very good, she will let me do it again sometime in the future. I have something to look forward to. More importantly, we all have something far more wonderful to look forward to, and this I can say from the pulpit. There is a day coming when righteousness and peace will kiss each other. Heavens knows that it so seldom happens now.

If you want to understand any passage of scripture the first thing that you do is to understand the situation that prompted it. But there is nothing here that suggests what that was, there were so many situations that it could fit in the history of Israel. God had done something wonderful and shown his favor, but now the psalmist was uncertain where they stood with him. Circumstances seemed to shout at them that their friend had now become their enemy. It is a situation that is common to many of us at some time, when things don't go as we hoped, but not everyone has had the blessing of seeing, as the Psalmist did, through the haze of the present to a clear vision of the future.

As I read this psalm I was struck with a contradiction. First salvation has been achieved. In verse 2 we read, "You forgave the iniquity of your people and covered all their sins." But as soon as he reflects on what God has done in the past, he plunges into the almost despair of the present reality in verses five to seven, 5"Will you be angry with us forever? Will you prolong your anger through all generations? 6 Will you not revive us again, that your people may rejoice in you? 7 Show us your unfailing love, Lord, and grant us your salvation."

My friends, do you remember when Jesus made you his own? Do you remember when he washed away your sins? Do you remember the joy of your first love for him? Yet it is so easy to take our eyes away, for circumstances to overtake us and even to doubt that we are Christ's. Are there any here who question or have questioned whether you are still walking with the one you called your savior? Have you sought for forgiveness and questioned whether it was given? "Have I behaved myself and been very, very good?" you might have asked. You would not have been alone.

Many Jewish congregations read this psalm on the Sabbath following the Day of Atonement, that day when sins are theoretically forgiven but before the rains come in Israel. These rains appeared to symbolize the visible proof that their sins actually have been washed away. Are you waiting for a tangible evidence that your God still loves you as on the day he first made you his?

Lord, You showed favor to Your land;
You restored the fortunes of Jacob.
2 You forgave the guilt of Your people;
You covered all their sin. Selah
3 You withdrew all Your fury;
You turned away from Your burning anger.
4 Restore us, God of our salvation,
And cause Your indignation toward us to cease.
5 Will You be angry with us forever?
Will You prolong Your anger to all generations?
6 Will You not revive us again,
So that Your people may rejoice in You?
7 Show us Your mercy, Lord,
And grant us Your salvation.

Psalm 85

There is one word that is repeated in the first half of the psalm, and that is "return." Just like the cycle of salvation or restoration and troubles coming in wave after wave, five times the word is mentioned.

7 I will hear what God the Lord will say;
For He will speak peace to His people, to His godly ones;
And may they not turn back to foolishness.
9 Certainly His salvation is near to those who fear Him,
That glory may dwell in our land.

The last section is very different, as one Jewish writer said, "But there is only one such use in the final section, which is "not return," as the cycle ends. The speaker suggests that God's ultimate intention is to overcome the cycle, to move to a new existence, which is most poetically and beautifully expressed."

There is a section of Christianity that appears to look at what it can get out of Jesus in this world, name it and claim it, blab it and grab it. I drive a Rolls Royce because Jesus would have driven a roller and I, like him, have a Rolls Royce size faith, after all, Jesus wore designer clothes and needed a treasurer. Someone told me a few weeks ago that Tenthill Baptist Church has in the past been called the church with the expensive cars. Well perhaps, but if that section of the church is right, our faith is seriously lacking due to the shortage of Bentleys in the car park. If we are living in poverty, we are outside of God's will. If you are sick, it is because you don't have enough faith, but my friends, this is all temporary. It will all pass away, your health and your sickness, your wealth, and your poverty. Don't put your confidence in the good things God has blessed you with. My heart is for the third world as you know; a Rolls Royce faith? They are thankful for their daily bread, and many have to ask for it every day. Make no mistake; what we are doing with Pastor Richard (who we support in India,) is a good thing.

But how do we cope with what is going on. Ted, tell me HOW? I can't tell you how, but I can tell you WHY we cope. That is not some cheap throwaway line, I was paraphrasing Victor Frankl, a famous Jewish neurologist and psychiatrist and an Auschwitz survivor. He ran the suicide watch in that hell hole, so I suppose he has earned the right to be listened to. He knew, as we must, that a day is coming when

Love and faithfulness meet together.
Righteousness and peace kiss each other.

You might say to me "Ted, couldn't you find a Christian to quote?" Well perhaps but I make no apologies. When I was writing my book, *Pain and a Powerful God*, I came across one of his gems of wisdom that really helped me through a very tough church situation. Some of you have also had to endure things you would have rather not, and I will share it with you. He said "The one thing you can't take away from me is the way I choose to respond to what you do to me. The last of one's freedoms is to choose one's attitude in any given circumstance." Not even an SS guard could take that freedom from him. How church drama affects me is no one's responsibility but my own, but I am digressing.

Love and faithfulness meet together;
Righteousness and peace kiss each other.

When two young people who are desperately in love have been separated for a long time, I am told that they can think of nothing else but the day they will be reunited. What happens on the day they are reunited? Do they sit down as Rachel, and I do in our advancing years and have a cup of tea? I think not, I am sure they hug and kiss. Love and faithfulness, righteousness and peace have been separated for too long. Lord hasten the day when they will be reunited in the glorious kingdom of your Son.

Here we have four of the most significant Hebrew words though I am not going to attempt to pronounce them correctly from the pulpit, and there are some sounds that simply should not come from a pulpit. The first is *hesed* or love, then *'Emet* or faithfulness, *tzedek* or righteousness, and *shalom* or peace. Our faith is one that has great ideas, and great promises and, despite difficulties has a wonderful present because of our Lord's presence.

I spoke about the word *Hesed* when I preached on Ruth. I showed a table which lists the way this word has been translated in different English versions. It is not a simple equivalent for love. One writer said "Hesed is not used to express the feeling between man and his fellowman but between people who are in close relationship to each other." He believed it to be a "strong and persistent attitude and is not dissolved by death." This view says that "Hesed was not basically mercy but loyalty to covenant obligations." It was described this way; God by grace chose to bind himself to his people in a covenant relationship. This set in place a cycle of mutual obligation. You can see that in this Psalm, God has forgiven them through his *hesed*, but they have been foolish, and they are pleading in desperation to see that *hesed* again. Is this your relationship with your savior?

Make no mistake. The covenant given through Moses was glorious. In 2 Corinthians 3:7 we read, "Now if the ministry that brought death, which was engraved in letters on stone, came with glory, so that the Israelites

Psalm 85

could not look steadily at the face of Moses because of its glory, transitory though it was."

But this wasn't the only covenant in the Old Testament, there is also the covenant given to Abraham in Genesis 15, the covenant with a man whose faith was credited to him as righteousness. This covenant helps us understand the glorious ministry of the Spirit.

> 9 So He said to him, "Bring Me a three-year-old heifer, a three-year-old female goat, a three-year-old ram, a turtledove, and a young pigeon." 10 Then he brought all these to Him and cut them in two and laid each half opposite the other; but he did not cut the birds. 11 And birds of prey came down upon the carcasses, and Abram drove them away.]
>
> 12 Now when the sun was going down, a deep sleep fell upon Abram; and behold, terror and great darkness fell upon him. 13 Then God said to Abram, "Know for certain that your descendants will be strangers in a land that is not theirs, where they will be enslaved and oppressed for four hundred years. 14 But I will also judge the nation whom they will serve, and afterward they will come out with many possessions. 15 As for you, you shall go to your fathers in peace; you will be buried at a good old age. 16 Then in the fourth generation they will return here, for the wrongdoing of the Amorite is not yet complete."
>
> 17 Now it came about, when the sun had set, that it was very dark, and behold, a smoking oven and a flaming torch appeared which passed between these pieces. 18 On that day the Lord made a covenant with Abram,

Here there was no mutual obligation. The idea was that the two people making a covenant would walk between the animals that had been dismembered. The dreadful sight of the butchered animals would say, "So be it unto you if you break the covenant." But this time only one walked through that gruesome path. Abraham was put into a deep sleep and could do nothing except receive the blessings. This was not a covenant of mutual responsibility. In the same way, my friends, there were no passengers on the cross when a thick and dreadful darkness came over this earth.

What covenant do you live under? Is it one of mutual responsibility, of behaving yourself and being very, very good so you will earn a future reward, or one of God's responsibilities? Who was it that drew you when you were not his friend? Who was it that changed your heart? Who was it that has led you to this day? Who was it that has held you close to himself?

Who will it be that takes you to himself when you take your last breath? It's grace, not goodness, not reward!

But what about that word 'emet? You are probably going to say, "What possible interest can the meaning of an ancient Hebrew word be to the church in the potato field in twenty-first century." To which I can only say, "Amen brother," quite literally, "Amen." We say it every time we pray.

The root from which 'emet is derived from is 'aman which has many other derivatives, the best known of these is 'amen. This word we use at the end of our prayers to this very day is used to express "certainty and assurance" that what we have prayed will come to pass. When we pray, do our words just go up and hit the ceiling or, do we have certainty and assurance that they pass through to the very throne of Almighty God? Other derivatives are used to describe faith and faithfulness. Back in 1972 when I first studied theology, the big debate in the Church of Christ College was whether the age of miracles had passed. When we think of the remarkable answers to prayer here,[1] who is going to stand up and discourage us from asking great things from our loving Savior?

In the movie *The Blues Brothers*, Elwood asks: "What kind of music do you usually have here?" And the reply was, "Oh, we got both kinds. We got country and western." But it isn't two; it's one thought that takes two words to express; other examples are warm and cozy, sick and tired, good and loud. In the same way God's love and his faithfulness are linked as in the example from Psalm 25:10, "All the paths of the Lord are faithfulness and truth to those who comply with His covenant and His testimonies," just as we are to be linked in love and faithfulness to our wife or husband. What is wonderful here in our text is that human and divine qualities are blurred.

What of righteousness and peace? God has promised peace or wellbeing. He promised it to his Old Testament saints as well as his New Testaments saints. But how can that peace be complete when righteousness is absent from the land? But our writer saw that they will come together and kiss like long absent lovers. God's righteousness that looks down from heaven will be our righteousness.

Our psalmist has gone from a shepherd or a pastor interceding for his people to become a prophet of a glorious future. I am only an old sawmiller but this morning I dare to declare to you a prophet's vision, our Lord will return. Your farms produce weeds so easily now, but the day is coming when

---

1. Some of these are recorded in my book of testimonies from the church, *So Much Blood*.

Psalm 85

11 Truth sprouts from the earth,
And righteousness looks down from heaven.
12 Indeed, the Lord will give what is good,
And our land will yield its produce.
Father, hasten the day of your son's return when:
10 Love and faithfulness meet together;
righteousness and peace kiss each other.

20

My Socks Tell the Gospel

Background

This communion address was given on Father's Day which prompted its content.

Address

Well, it's Father's Day. Hands up those who got underpants for a present? Hands up who got socks? (By this point most of the men had their hands up.) Now you might think that that is boring, but not when Rachel (my wife) buys them. (At this point I pulled up my trouser legs and showed that I had one red and one gold colored sock.)

Now you might think that socks like these are unusual, but they aren't. I have another pair at home exactly the same! Last year I received a pair where one was black, and the other was white. Where does she purchase socks like this, Myers, Target, K Mart? No, Koorong[1] for they tell the story of the gospel.

You see my heart was once black with sin but because of the blood of our dear Lord Jesus, he made it white as snow. One day I am going to walk streets of gold in his kingdom.

---

1. An Australian chain of Christian bookstores.

21

Life's Storms

Background

MURRAY WINDOLF WAS A young member of the Tenthill Baptist Church and is a layman like me. This sermon has come out of the struggles he and his wife Peta have experienced due to the serious health issues of a family member. His sermon is fresh and unusual, and I would have been elated to have been able to preach like this at his age.

Text: Mark 6:45–52.

⁴⁵ *And immediately Jesus had His disciples get into the boat and go ahead of Him to the other side, to Bethsaida, while He Himself dismissed the crowd.* ⁴⁶ *And after saying goodbye to them, He left for the mountain to pray.*

⁴⁷ *When it was evening, the boat was in the middle of the sea, and He was alone on the land.* ⁴⁸ *Seeing them straining at the oars—for the wind was against them—at about the fourth watch of the night, He came to them, walking on the sea; and He intended to pass by them.* ⁴⁹ *But when they saw Him walking on the sea, they thought that it was a ghost, and they cried out;* ⁵⁰ *for they all saw Him and were terrified. But immediately He spoke with them and said to them, "Take courage; it is I, do not be afraid."* ⁵¹ *Then He got into the boat with them, and the wind stopped; and they were utterly astonished,* ⁵²

for they had not gained any insight from the incident of the loaves, but their hearts were hardened.

I love to fish, but sometimes the thought is better than the reality. One seemingly fine day my brother and father-in-law decided we would go fishing with a friend over at Bribie Island. It was a beautiful day, perfect for fishing. I couldn't wait. Standing at the loading ramp I thought this is going to be great, it doesn't get much better than this, what could go wrong? So off we go. Finally, we get there, 50 kilometers offshore. After about an hour of fishing the wind starts to pick up and so did the size of the waves. Not everyone enjoyed this change. This was obvious by the sudden attraction to the side of the boat in a bent over position. The swell got so bad that you couldn't even stand up, so it was time to leave and find calm waters.

That's how life can be. One day everything is in control with not a care in the world and then, bang, your world can begin to fall apart. I don't share this topic lightly for it is something I've been processing for a while. Problems, we all have them. Do we believe God is in control? Is he all we need? Will we be okay if our fears were to happen?

I want to share with you today a little bit of what I know and believe about the life of Jesus in me today. I know he is alive and living in us today. We are not to imitate the life of Christ but participate in it. It turns boring old dos and don'ts into a fruitful life.

In Mark chapter 6, Jesus has just finished feeding the 5000 and he sends the disciples to the next town by themselves. He stays back and then spends time alone. While he is praying, he watches the boat go out and get stuck in a storm. The disciples struggle and strain for hours, facing the storm by themselves. Finally, Jesus walks out to them on the water and calms the sea.

I want to talk about this Bible passage and how we react in the storms of life, big or small. Where does Jesus fit in? What is a learnt habit, and a normal reaction is not always right?

Jesus knew that the calm water wouldn't last, but he still sent them out knowing exactly what was coming up. Same with us in our lives, he knows exactly what is coming our way. Personally, I think it's for our best that we don't know what's coming. Nothing comes in our lives without firstly God giving it permission. Whatever he permits, he also provides more than enough grace for the circumstance. He is never far away, just as he was with the disciples.

Life's Storms

Sometimes life is smooth, but it can change in a split second. We all have had those phone calls that something has happened to someone. Most of the storms of life we are faced with are not as dramatic or life threatening as the storm in this passage. Often the everyday events of life, work, family, money are the most exhausting storms.

For example, trying to fill a lawn mower without a funnel. The funnel is used to point the petrol in the right direction, the fuel tank. I believe these everyday problems are a funnel to point us to our need of God in a moment-by-moment life. He sent the disciples out to test their faith, to show them where they needed to put their faith. God uses these problems to develop his relationship with us. He didn't just save us from Hell he wants to save us moment by moment by abiding in him which can be found in John 15.

Do we row our boat in the face of trouble and stress? In verse forty-eight Jesus saw the disciples straining on the boat. He watched them for hours. It says he went to them at the fourth watch of the night, that's four o'clock in the morning. He watched them wondering why they weren't calling out to him. They had just witnessed a miracle yet still their focus was on their trouble not their savior. Are we any different? Do we row our own boat in the face of trouble and stress? We all have our own ways of coping. Do we get cranky and short with those close to us? We wonder where Jesus is and why these things happen to us, even question him.

The bigger the problem the more we row. Spinning out of control. Personally, under stress my first reaction is to take control, not trusting Jesus at all. When I have a lot to do at work, I spend all my time focusing on the problem. Sometimes when people ask for a job to be done all I can see are the complications of the job. If we look at a pencil closely and bring it closer and closer to our eyes, it consumes all our focus. It is the same with our problems. If we start thinking about the problem, before you know it, that's all we can think and feel.

In Jonah 2:8 it says, "Those who cling to worthless idols forfeit the grace that could be theirs." The verse says, "Worthless idols," we all have them, it's what we turn to in a time of need; it could be anxiety, stress, anger. All are habits, they all are worthless, as they do not offer any grace for the situation. Personally, I've missed out on many hours of sleep because I've opted to stress and worry about things rather than believing that Jesus is enough for the circumstance. We carry life's burdens, and we live a defeated life. That is all because we do not believe in Jesus' sufficiency. This is the same unbelief that kept the Israelites out of the promised land. Do we believe Jesus is in control and does care?

Jesus meets us where we are. He walked on water to the boat. Jesus will come to us in our storms. He doesn't want you to get yourself sorted out and then we can talk, he comes to us via our problems. Problems or storms may be anything caused by self or others, but Jesus allows these things into our life and wants us to believe in his moment-by-moment salvation. The enemy can't stop people from being saved eternally, but he tries to stop Christians being saved moment by moment. He does this by selling us a lie, whispering in our ears causing us to doubt that Jesus will help, and we end up working harder. Defeat is a common problem amongst Christians because they are not trusting in Jesus to be their victory because of the lies. A man in a gutter was told by a Christian that he needed Jesus. He turned around and said, "No thanks I've got enough problems." He obviously knew some very confused Christians who had let life beat them. The secret is to invite Jesus into all of life and watch him work his victorious life through you, but this doesn't mean hardship will disappear.

The noise of the storm can be deafening. The disciples were surprised to see Jesus. They didn't expect him to turn up. We don't recognize his voice or his presence. They were consumed with the noise of the storm. It is hard to hear in the storm. If we believe and stop striving and making noise, we will hear him say, "Take courage, it is me" (6:50). I was recently sitting in in the emergency ward at the hospital and there were two interesting characters waiting. One was drunk and the other was mentally unstable. The unstable one said he hears voices and the drunk man wisely said, *"We all hear voices, it's what you do with them."* We need to learn to know His voice. The first thing is to stop and listen instead of thrashing around. Ask to hear His voice in the circumstance.

We have two choices in life's storm, you let him in, or he walks on by. This doesn't mean the circumstances will change, but YOU will change in the circumstances. In Isaiah 26:3–4 it says, "You will keep in perfect peace him whose mind is steadfast because he trusts in you." What a difference this makes in my life every day! This is not a one-time fix, but each time I am learning to get back on track quicker.

Belief can be a habit. I admit in the big or small troubles my first reaction isn't always to focus on Jesus. I have learnt an easy way to keep focusing on Jesus is to simply pray, "Lord, this is too big for me, it's going to be exciting to see what you do." My wife and I have sat next to our youngest daughter in hospital for many days with many worries, and yes things do get too big, the only thing to do is to say, "It's all yours Lord." Can I encourage you to let Jesus into the circumstances, let him in the boat. I would rather sail than row any day!

22

The Parable of Hank

Background

CHRIS MEYER IS ANOTHER capable layman at Tenthill Baptist Church. He has competed in rodeos since 1984 in Australia and the USA in bronc riding and roping events. He has worked as a horse breaker and trainer for big companies and had his own business.

Chris, along with his wife Georgi and their four children spent fifteen years with Athletes in Action serving as a Chaplain on the professional rodeo circuit and delivering life skills and value seminars in schools around Queensland. He was, at the time, working at Emu Gully, a campsite at Helidon, and was, the Chairman of the Board of Directors for the National Rodeo Association. His "Parable of Hank" was delivered in the potato field in 2013

Chris Meyer

The Parable of Hank

Hank is a five-year-old, brown quarter horse gelding. I bought Hank three years ago for a particular purpose, to be a rope horse. I could have brought a more finished horse to present this talk but, as Hank is still learning, he would better demonstrate the principles I want to convey. I also could have used my competition saddle and bridle but that would have given the impression that this was a show. I have used my work tack to show that this horse is still under construction, he's still learning skills, obedience, and trust.

Chris with Hank

One of Jesus' sayings that I've most struggled with in my life is, "Blessed are the meek," (Matt 5:5). In the English language meek is a very weak word and as a professional rodeo cowboy it didn't sit well with me or my understanding of Jesus and his manhood. However, when I learnt that the word Jesus used for meekness in the Greek was also the word used for breaking in a horse, I understood exactly what Jesus meant. Hence, *The Parable of Hank*.

There is an old hymn that says, "Trust and obey for there's no other way, to be happy in Jesus but to trust and obey." Trust and obedience are crucial for training a horse. It is essential that the two go together. Some people when they handle a horse will concentrate more on the trust element, wanting the horse to be their friend and to love them. However, trust without discipline isn't love, it develops a self-centered horse that becomes overpowering. A horse that won't listen, that demands its own way, becomes very difficult to handle because they have no respect. In the horse world we call an obnoxious horse, "spoilt."

On the other hand, a horse that has been forced to comply and do what he is told without building trust, that horse will be either timid, too frightened to do anything in case they get reprimanded or become "snaky" and look to get back at the handler whenever they can. Either way this horse won't give you his heart because he hasn't been taught in relationship.

A master trainer will seek to build relationship through the horse by using both elements of trust and obedience. The trainer will ask for compliance to a simple task, the horse might strain against it or even retaliate. The trainer will patiently wait until the horse complies and then reward the behavior with release. I might put pressure on a rein for example asking the horse to move his head to the left. The horse will fight against it, wanting to go their own way. However, when they finally succumb to the pressure and give their head, immediately I will release the pressure and they will learn that it is easier to obey. As the horse starts to obey the commands to steer, they also learn to trust in the one who gives the command. As a trainer, sometimes you need to be really firm or even tough if the horse wants to be aggressive. However as soon as that horse gives the slightest bit, you reward them with release. Horses learn by pressure and release, trust, and obedience.

An essential part of building any relationship is effective communication. Communication involves listening as well as speaking. A horse, if we are willing to listen and understand their language, will tell us pretty clearly how they are feeling. They obviously don't speak with their mouth but with their actions. Therefore, if I am to win the horses trust, I will communicate to him by asking him to give an area of his body in obedience. A horse will demonstrate his behavior with his face. By the position of his ears, eyes, nostrils, whether he looks at me or away, he will be showing me how he feels about me i.e., nervous, annoyed, etc. With his shoulders he will let me know his attitude. When I am leading or lunging a horse, if he is obnoxious, he will drop his shoulder in on me and bully me, so he doesn't have to give me his head. If he is nervous, he will point his face at me and keep his shoulders and rump in a straight line behind him. A horse has the most power when he is in a straight line from head to tail with his head and tail

The Parable of Hank

up. When you move their shoulder away and hold the lead, they must give their head. As they move their head toward me and find release with the rope, they learn that when they give to pressure there is a reward. In this way I can work on his attitude/shoulder and as a result I gain control of his behavior/face. Often in the Old Testament God calls Israel a stiff-necked people, meaning that they want to go their own way, maintain power, and control and not soften their will and follow the master.

The last area I want to gain control of is the horse's hip because the hip represents his heart. When I move the horse's shoulder away, he will give me his head, but his head will still be in the air. If I push the rump forward into his head, his head will lower and the back will become rounded, a sign of submission. Once a horse submits his will, I have his life. Then the only limit to what this horse can achieve will be my abilities as a trainer, or the horse' physical agility.

When I am riding a horse, my hands will control his head and my feet will control his body. Using my hands and feet I demonstrated this control by putting Hank into all sorts of positions. We performed a side pass, rollback, spin, sliding stop, back up, etc. As the horse becomes more proficient at the various tasks the cues become less obvious. The relationship grows to the point where the horse can feel what the trainer desires and responds accordingly. At this point the relationship brings much joy and pleasure to the trainer, and great reward for the horse.

When I bought Hank, I had a special purpose for him, to be a rope horse. As a rodeo cowboy I compete for trophies and money. To be successful I need a great horse. While I have to be able to rope well, my horse is worth ninety percent of my run. In the team roping event that I compete in; one cowboy catches the steer by the horns; he's called a header. Once the header has the steer caught, he takes a wrap around his saddle horn with his rope and turns the steer to the left. It is then the second part of the team (the healer's) job to catch the steer by the back feet. Once the feet are caught the heel horse stops, the head horse will then face the steer and then the clock stops and the fastest time wins. You see, it doesn't matter how good a roper I am if my horse won't run into position, I'll never be able to catch the steer. I need a horse that will listen to me and let me put him exactly where I need him to be.

Sermons from a Potato Field

Chris roping his daughter Kate

I then demonstrated a roping run using my eleven-year-old daughter Kate as a steer. She ran a pattern just like a steer would. I rode Hank into position and caught Kate by the feet. I bought Hank for a bargain; I got him for $1000. He would be worth five or six times that amount now. When he finishes his training and I start competing on him he could be worth twice that amount. What changed his worth? As the old song says, it was, "The touch of the master's hand."

I then dismounted and unclipped a rein and put it around Hank's near side leg. With slight pressure I was able to lead Hank forward with his leg. I then put the rein around his back legs, and I was able to lead him with his back legs. I did this to show that I want every area of this pony's life. I want him to respond to me under any pressure.

The Parable of Hank

Hank following Chris

I then walked off and Hank followed me, wherever I went. At one point he stopped and had a little look around. I could have got all upset that my horse was making me look bad in front of everyone but that's not how the principle of grace works. I just went back gave him a pat on his nose, put some pressure on his bridle and asked to follow me. I want him to learn that I am the best place to be. This can put me in a precarious position, if the horse gets a fright he will jump, without thinking, to the safest place, me.

The amazing thing about Jesus is that when he called his disciples to follow him in Mark 1, he didn't require them to be perfect but simply asks them to follow. As they did, he led them to a leper and they saw compassion, then to a paralytic and found forgiveness, and then to the house of Levi a tax collector and they saw acceptance. As they followed Jesus, they saw him bring hope, justice, and grace into people's lives and witnessed the Kingdom of God in action. The more their relationship grew the more Jesus required of their commitment to him. Years later when they were persecuted even to death, where did they jump? They jumped into the arms of the Master.

Hank is blindfolded and without a bridle

But that's not enough. At this point I took Hank's bridle off. What happens when all the things that we rely on for security are gone? But even that is not enough; I then put a blind fold on Hank. What happens when we get blindsided by something beyond our control? Our partner leaves, we lose our job, the loss of a loved one, cancer. I then mounted Hank. A young horse without a bridle and blindfolded, this could be disastrous. As we step into the unknown one thing becomes clear to Hank, that even though things are difficult I am still here. In the midst of uncertainty, the master is still here. We're reminded of a promise, "I'll never leave you or forsake you."

The Parable of Hank

Hank completely trusts Chris

We start to trot around, how will Hank know the way? Well, I am the way. Even though the queues are different as long as he listens to me, I will guide him away from danger and keep him safe. We make a circle each way and then stop and back up.

Some people might say that this horse has blind faith. But he's not blind, he simply trusts in the one who can see.

Hank surrenders to Chris

I then put a halter on Hank and laid him down. I sat on his shoulder; Hank has surrendered his life to me. Here is the expression of meekness fully realized as this horse with the power to kill me if he so chose to, surrenders his life to me. Trusting in my goodness that I will never do him harm, he learns through obedience to give me his heart. As he gives me his heart he is changed, touched by the master's hand.

My grandfather wrote a verse in the front of my first Bible when I was 10 years old, and it has served as a foundation throughout my life, "Trust in the Lord with all your heart and lean not to your own understanding; in all your ways acknowledge him, and he will make your paths straight" (Prov 3:5,6).

And that is, "The Parable of Hank!"

Source of Images

Figure 1	Eternity	Sardaka 09:13, 2 May 2008 (UTC), CC BY-SA 3.0 <http://creativecommons.org/licenses/by-sa/3.0/>, via Wikimedia Commons
Figure 3	Teddy Bear	Smithsonian Museum of Natural History, CC BY-SA 2.0 <https://creativecommons.org/licenses/by-sa/2.0>, via Wikimedia Commons
Figure 3	Light Horse memorial at Beersheba	צילום:ד"ר אבישי טייכר, CC BY 2.5 <https://creativecommons.org/licenses/by/2.5>, via Wikimedia Commons
Figure 4	Author somewhere exotic	Author
Figure 5	Stoa of Attalos	Author
Figure 6	Colum base	Shutterstock
Figure 7	Archbishop Sancroft	After Bernard Lens II, Public domain, via Wikimedia Commons
Figure 8	Chris Meyer	Chris Meyer
Figure 9	Chris with Hank	Author
Figure 10	Chris roping his daughter Kate	Author

Sermons from a Potato Field

Figure 11	Hank following Chris	Stanley Smith
Figure 12	Hank is blindfolded and without a bridle	Author
Figure 13	Hank completely trusts Chris	Stanley Smith
Figure 14	Hank surrenders to Chris	Author

www.ingramcontent.com/pod-product-compliance
Lightning Source LLC
Chambersburg PA
CBHW070919180426
43192CB00038B/1872